I0147211

Compassionate Mediation®

For Relationships at a Crossroad

How to Add
Passion to Your Marriage
or *Compassion* to Your Divorce

Linda Kroll

Therapist, Mediator, Attorney

Copyright 2017 © Linda Kroll

Published in the United States by Compassionate Communication, Inc. and CreateSpace.com

Throughout the book, I have used stories and examples designed to briefly help the reader understand the process. The stories are composites and the names have been changed to ensure confidentiality.

All rights reserved: No part of this book may be reproduced by any mechanical, photographic or electronic process, or in the form of a phonographic recording; nor may it be stored in a retrieval system, transmitted, or otherwise be copied for public or private use—other than "fair use" as brief quotations embodied in articles and reviews—without prior written permission of the author and publisher.

The author of this book is not providing legal or medical advice. The intent of the author is only to offer information of a general nature to help you in in your quest for emotional, financial, legal, and spiritual wellbeing. In the event you use any of the information in this book for yourself, the author and publisher assume no responsibility for your actions.

Edited by:
Leonard Sherp, lsherp@lscommunications.net
CJ Schepers, cjschepers@mac.com, cjschepers.com

Cover Illustration by:
Miraculous Divine Love © 2014 Colleen McGunnigle, SoulCenteredArt.com

Mandala by:
Paul Heussenstamm www.mandalas.com

Library of Congress Cataloging-in-Publication Data available upon request.
Linda Kroll
   Compassionate Mediation®: For Relationships at a Crossroad. How to Add *Passion* to Your Marriage or *Compassion* to Your Divorce Linda Kroll –
ISBN Tradepaper13: 978-0996735520
October, 2017
Printed in the United States of America

Dedication

With infinite thanks to
my beloved mother, Helen,
and my precious daughters,
Kimberly and Dana:

Your wisdom, humor, support, and
unconditional love inspire me always.

And to my devoted brother, Jerry:

For our lifetime of shared
guidance, love, and laughter.

Please get your FREE Compassionate Mediation® Toolkit
www.CMToolkit.com

Congratulations on taking a step to help heal and transform your relationship. *This book is interactive with links to videos to offer more guidance and support.*

I am thrilled to show you how to bring it to life. All the QR (Quick Response) codes throughout the book can be scanned with your Smartphone or iPad. Each of the videos is approximately two minutes long and you can scan them at your convenience.

If you have questions, please contact Support@LindaKroll.com.

How to Scan the QR Codes in This Book

Step 1: Download a *free* QR code reader onto your smartphone by searching the App Store.

Step 2: Tap the app once it has downloaded to your phone; this will open up the Reader. Tap again, and your camera will appear to be on.

Hover over the code you wish to scan, and the camera will automatically take a picture of the QR code; then your phone will be directed to the respective web page that contains each video message.

I look forward to connecting with you.

Compassionate Mediation® Training for Professionals
Please join me and learn more:
www.CompassionateMediationTraining.com

Table of Contents

Foreword   v
Relationship Survey   xi
Client Successes   xv
Appreciation   xxi
Introduction   xxvii

SECTION ONE
Compassionate Communication Begins with You

Chapter 1: Connect to Your Highest and Best SELF   1
Chapter 2: Understand and Love Your "Parts"   27
Chapter 3: 5 Steps to Get What You Want and Need   57
Chapter 4: Experience the Miracle of Empathy   65

SECTION TWO
Compassionate Mediation®
Become Your Own Best Advocate

Chapter 5: Explore All Your Options   97
Chapter 6: Learn Your Rights   113

SECTION THREE
Reduce Your Stress with Exquisite SELF-Care

Chapter 7: Tune In To Your SELF   145
Chapter 8: Let Go of Limiting Beliefs   171
Chapter 9: Unburden Your Inner Child   185

SECTION FOUR
Make Decisions from Your Highest SELF

Chapter 10: Add Passion to Your Relationship   191
Chapter 11: Add Compassion to a SELF-Led Divorce®   201
Chapter 12: Compassion for All   231

Compassionate Mediation® Introduction Video

http://LindaKroll.com/Compassionate-Mediation-Introduction

Compassionate Communication Video

http://LindaKroll.com/Compassionate-Mediation-Unhappy-Marriage

Foreword

When it comes to starting, maintaining, or ending a relationship, we are faced with a relentless and challenging dilemma. Our desire to be in a compassionate relationship, to commune with another person, and to connect our hearts has not wavered, yet, we either don't have the tools or don't know what tools to use to help us master the connections we all seek and hold meaningful two-way dialog.

As we look around, we observe more than half of the relationships around us aren't working out the way they were first envisioned. As our own relationships falter, we struggle for the words, techniques, or processes to bring clarity to our emotions, to have those difficult conversations, to heal the wounds so deeply etched in our heart, and to find the courage and compassion to move forward with grace and ease in our life.

In our personal relationships and in our marriages, we can struggle daily to say what we mean, to speak the truth, to be kind in our interactions, and to resolve conflict. We desperately strive to meet the needs of our heart – attention, affection, appreciation, and acceptance. Yet often, we are unsuccessful as our attempts to repair, shift, or evolve our own core relationship ends up creating resentment, hostility, anger, arguments, adversarial antagonists, and polarizing scenarios where we are left with only the legal system to impose its binding solutions on our lives.

Those finding themselves in such bizarre situations as they gaze across the courtroom from each other are left to wonder, "How did it come to this?" "How did we go from best friends to enemies?" "Why didn't we have the tools to solve this?"

Well, the tools have been around for millennia but they are not in the schoolbooks we carried from kindergarten through college. So critical to our survival and to the success of every relationship we enter into, these tools are rarely taught in bedrooms, classrooms, or boardrooms. Our society points the way but doesn't provide the training necessary to keep the relationship thriving or the compassionate path to ending it and moving on. That's why this book is so valuable and transformational.

Linda Kroll has been there - done that. She has been at the crossroads - walked through the fire and crawled through glass. She has emerged from darkness into light.

She has transmuted her life lessons into magnificent guidance for anyone looking to add passion to their marriage or compassion to their divorce. She has experienced both the personal and legal sides of divorce. She has endured the pain, disappointment, frustration, and sadness of separation. And in that process, she has mastered the art of mediation, guiding thousands through her professional mediation practice, her role as a therapist, her writing, and her online programs.

Her expertise is a fusion of her own life experience; working lovingly with her clients; and being a life-long student AND a powerful teacher of heart-healing and compassionate communication. Her brilliant understanding of emotions, conscious communication, timeless wisdom AND her knowledge of the steps to shift from stuck to celebration are all contained in *Compassionate Mediation® for Relationships at a Crossroad.*

I love Linda as a person. I honor her as a student of mine. And, I am in awe of her as a compassionate agent of healing and transformation in our modern world.

In these pages, Linda has crafted a roadmap of how to take your life to the next level. Keep reading! The journey will teach you that the light at the end of the tunnel is not the illusion… the tunnel is the illusion.

The light is real. It's yours for the asking. You are worthy of it… entitled to it. Peace in your mind and your heart is actually your birthright. And the pain you feel right now – which seems like it will never end— is actually only a few inches long. By turning the page and following Linda's guidance, you will be soothed, healed, and empowered to take your life to the next level. Enjoy.

—davidji
Best-selling author of *destressifying* and *Secrets of Meditation*
davidji.com

Compassionate Relationships Video

http://LindaKroll.com/Compassionate-Mediation-Relationship-Healing

Add Passion and Compassion Video

http://LindaKroll.com/Compassionate-Mediation

Relationship Survey

This survey will give you an overview of your partnership today. You can focus on your true feelings and begin to clarify your hopes for the future. You'll discover how you communicate, resolve conflict, parent your children, handle your finances, view intimacy, engage with family and friends, and meet the needs of your own heart. You'll realize what further support you'll need to create the relationship of your dreams.

Communication

I would like to be more connected.	Yes/No
I want my partner to change.	Yes/No
I don't think my partner wants to listen to me.	Yes/No
I don't want to listen to my partner.	Yes/No
I think we could both show more empathy.	Yes/No
I am often misunderstood.	Yes/No
I don't always share all of what I feel.	Yes/No
I shut down when I'm angry.	Yes/No
I act angry when I'm sad.	Yes/No
I want to learn a new way to communicate.	Yes/No

Conflict Resolution

I often feel frustrated.	Yes/No
I withdraw when I'm hurt.	Yes/No
We bicker a lot.	Yes/No
Our children hear us argue.	Yes/No
Our family feels the tension even when we don't fight.	Yes/No

Parenting

We're not on the same page.	Yes/No
I don't like the way my partner parents.	Yes/No
Our children play one against the other.	Yes/No
I do everything myself.	Yes/No
I feel alone.	Yes/No

Finances

I earn all of the money.	Yes/No
I wish my partner contributed more.	Yes/No
My partner spends too much.	Yes/No
I don't feel like an equal partner.	Yes/No
I want us to agree on a budget.	Yes/No

Intimacy

I wish my partner were more affectionate.	Yes/No
I am not completely satisfied with my sex life.	Yes/No
I don't like sex.	Yes/No
I'm not attracted to my partner.	Yes/No
I don't feel attractive to my partner.	Yes/No
I withhold sex when I'm angry or hurt.	Yes/No
I've thought about having an affair.	Yes/No
I'm having (or have had) an affair.	Yes/No
I don't trust my partner.	Yes/No

Family and Friends

We spend too much time with his/her family.	Yes/No
We spend too much time with his/her friends.	Yes/No
We don't do enough socially together.	Yes/No
His/her friends/family don't like me.	Yes/No

Needs of the Heart

I wish I felt more acceptance.	Yes/No
I long for more affection.	Yes/No
I don't get enough attention.	Yes/No
I don't feel like I'm truly appreciated.	Yes/No

TOTALS ___Yes ___No

Based on the number of times you answered "Yes":

0–5	You have a beautiful relationship!
6–10	You're two individuals. No one is perfect.
11–15	Counseling would be useful.
16–20	Counseling will be invaluable.
21–25	You can create a new relationship with the right support.
26–30	New habits need to be created.
31–35	Your pain can be healed.
36–40	Are you showing up as your best SELF?

I wish that I could meet with you personally, and perhaps someday we will. In the mean time, I'd like to offer you the same information I've provided to thousands of men and women over the last 20 years. Sometimes individuals will come to me for counseling, but the root of their distress is their relationship. Often a couple will see me for marital counseling, with both of them committed to creating a better relationship together. In other cases, a couple planning a divorce will pursue mediation, and in the process of learning how to communicate with compassion, they are able to create a new relationship together.

Compassionate Communication enables you to connect to your best SELF, let go of limiting beliefs, heal burdens from your past, and relate from your heart. You can use **Compassionate Mediation**® to decide whether to focus your efforts on creating a new and better **Compassionate Relationship** with your partner, or to realize it's better to go your separate ways with a **Compassionate or SELF-Led Divorce**®.

This book is for you if you're not sure what you want to do. Whether you think you'd like to keep your family together or you're certain you want a divorce, I offer you the same process that I'd give you in person. So let's imagine we're doing this together—which is a possibility--and I'll help you plan for your future based on what *you want and need* from your *highest SELF*.

Help for Individuals and Couples Video

http://LindaKroll.com/Compassionate-Mediation-Compassionate-Communication

Reach Out for Help Video

http://LindaKroll.com/Sharing-My-Story

Client Successes

"We're building an entirely new marriage."

"I resisted leaving for years with two young kids and limited finances, the idea of leaving felt almost as bad as staying. By the end of our first session, we were able to strip away some of the old resentments and junk to have a glimpse of the person we fell in love with all those years ago. After a few short months, we are no longer thinking of ending our marriage. Linda is helping us build an entirely new marriage. She is a Godsend and is helping me to love myself, love my husband, and love my life. What a treasure."
—Liz

"I came to Linda seeking mediated divorce documents and came out with nothing but peace and hope."

"Linda's unwavering pursuit of compassion and dogged exploration into the emotional history of both our lives was incredibly revelatory. I came to understand how little I understood myself emotionally as well as how much pain I had suppressed, hidden, or avoided. I was able then to see my wife as a person to be respected, instead of a problem to be solved, and now am party to perhaps the best divorce the world has seen. My relationship with my ex-wife now is better than it ever was when we were married. Our child has performed a full reversal of negative behaviors to become a desired friend, colleague, and leader in her social circles."
—Jeremy

"I've experienced significant improvements in my relationship with my husband and children."

"When you're stuck or unhappy in your closest relationships, it's easy to lose faith in yourself and in life. Linda helped me to regain that trust. Even though my family was unwilling to participate in the process, Linda taught me new ways to approach old patterns…I've experienced significant improvements in my relationship with my husband and children. I was enduring a contentious marriage and now both of us have reached a place of reconciliation. For me, this is the key: Linda guides you to re-frame your story with compassion for yourself AND all your significant relationships, even the most difficult and hurtful. Thank you with all my heart, Linda!"

—Mary

"She has guided me to safely unburden past wounds "

"I will forever be grateful I found Linda to help me on my journey to SELF. She has guided me to lovingly and safely unburden past wounds and traumas, and fill it with self-love, self-acceptance and self-forgiveness."

—Kathy

"Linda's process gave me a sense of clarity and peace."

"Linda has a gigantic tool box. Her ability to pick the proper tools at the proper moments was ingenious. I have experienced Linda in groups and alone. Both proved to be invaluable. Climbing up the mountain with Linda's support, and being able to see what was in front of me, gave me a sense of clarity and peace."

—Joan

"Linda guided us mindfully through the impact of divorce."

"My (former) husband and I owned a business together and worked together every day. We wanted to dissolve our marriage but not lose our company in the process. Linda helped us sort out the dysfunctional parts of the relationship from the parts of our relationship that still worked and we wanted to retain, allowing us to continue to work together, successfully, for years. She helped us separate from each other in a mutually respectable way so that I could move past my anger and disappointment in the failed relationship.

She also helped us stay focused on what was really important: our 3 year old child, making him the center of most of our decisions, asking ourselves what was best for him as we wrote our joint parenting agreement. When our son attended a group for kids of divorced parents at his school, they thought he was fantasizing when he told the counselor his parents worked together every day. Not only was Linda able to guide and advice us mindfully through the psychological and physical impact of divorce, but also the legal aspects, helping us as she wrote our divorce decree to suit our needs."
—Gina

"Linda helped me love all 'Parts' of my SELF!"

"Entering my 50s, my roles as a mother, wife, daughter, sister, and SELF were challenging and exciting. I was looking for balance, and a stronger validation of SELF. I wanted to maintain my roles from a place of truth. Linda guided me, bringing all my Parts to the table, and helped me to separate, change, love, and validate them all."
—Deb

"I am breaking free from destructive patterns."

"In just one session with Linda Kroll, I gained insight into a stumbling block in my relationship that I thought was impassable. Her clarity and intelligence cut through my defenses allowing me to see the ways in which I was sabotaging myself. She is a serious and effective therapist who continues to give me the courage to face my painful past and the tools to break free from destructive patterns. I am very grateful for her presence in my life and awed by her extraordinary skill. "
—Carol

"With Linda's caring guidance, I moved forward with peace and strength."

"When I was first referred to Linda, I felt sad, scared, alone and extremely confused. With Linda's caring guidance, I learned ways to cope with what was happening with my life and how to move forward with peace and strength. She showed me options I didn't know existed. This helped me feel so much more in control of my actions and decisions and allowed me to be a strong role model for my children. Life is so much better…I now face each day with excitement, strength, and peace."
—Ann

"Linda is my Zoloft®!"

"Whenever I remember the caring presence and compassionate direction she brought to our sessions, I feel more calm. Linda is my Zoloft®!"
—Rick

"I learned there could be a compassionate divorce."

Before working with Linda, I was trying to figure out the direction that I should take individually, how to decide whether a divorce was the most logical option for me and my family, and first and foremost the best way to handle these challenges while providing the best outcome possible for our daughter, who did nothing to deserve any of the changes that were taking place.

I imagine that working with me and my spouse was quite challenging as we both brought a lot with us while dealing with intense life issues Once the difficult decisions were further along, there was space to let concepts into my mind and heart of empathy and compassion. Linda always seemed to maintain an ability to stay above the fray, and she taught me how to come from my Highest Self. I feel that I understood the meaning of Highest Self immediately, yet before being introduced to that concept by Linda, I don't think that I operated from that place often enough.

I am now working toward living my best life, from my Highest Self, looking for good things for myself, my newly structured family, and for the greater good in my business and personal life.
—Paul

Hope and Healing Video

http://LindaKroll.com/Compassionate-Mediation-Couples-Counseling

Explore Your Options Video

http://LindaKroll.com/Compassionate-Mediation-Individual-Counseling

Appreciation and Acknowledgments

For All My Family and Friends

I am blessed with an extraordinary, loving family and a beloved circle of friends. Every one of you is an integral part of the fabric of my life. Fortunately, there are too many to list, but you all know who you are. You have exemplified devotion, compassion and love, and there are not enough words to show my heartfelt gratitude.

I am also grateful to my former husband and his family, who have graced my life for decades. I am thankful for all the love we have known and for the magnificent children and grandchildren we share.

Special Thanks to My Clients

I am grateful to all my family, friends, colleagues, teachers, guides, mentors, and also to my present and former clients. Their courageous honesty and willingness to heal and transform have inspired me for over twenty years. I am privileged to have been a part of their lives and have them be a part of mine.

And now I am honored to have YOU here to share the skills of Compassionate Mediation so you can bring more peace and happiness to your life.

Let the healing begin.

Gratitude to My Mentors and Colleagues

For over 20 years, I have practiced Internal Family Systems (IFS) Therapy, founded by Richard Schwartz, my mentor and friend. Dick first introduced me to this integrative approach of SELF and Parts over twenty years ago. In the IFS model of psychotherapy, **Self-Leadership** is characterized by eight "C qualities": compassion, calmness, clarity, curiosity, confidence, courage, creativity, and connectedness. I later added "grateful" to the list, and I'm sure there are more words to describe that feeling of being present, without judgment or agenda or need to control. As an IFS therapist, I knew the importance of healing pain from the past and staying present with SELF energy.

I had always had my own personal spiritual connection, however Compassionate Mediation is helpful no matter what you believe. The idea of "SELF" became for me that direct connection to the divine, or Divine within, embodying all those eight "C qualities" listed above.

When the Chopra Center came to Chicago in 2008, and I heard Deepak Chopra, David Simon, and davidji talk about *higher consciousness* and the idea of Brahman or Oneness, I also identified with those concepts. I continued my quest to lead a more spiritual life that was not led by my ego's needs or desires.

Their references to "higher SELF" and "higher consciousness." resonated with me. Both Dick Schwartz and the Chopra team spoke of the "wave and the ocean," which to me incorporated the individual wave or ego (self) with the vastness of the ocean (SELF). As the Sufi poet Rumi has said, *"You are not just the drop in the ocean, but the ocean in a drop."*

As a Chopra Center University student, and later a Master Teacher of Meditation, Yoga and Ayurveda, I learned how our awareness—or level of consciousness—affects our ability to relate with more compassion and creativity to others.

Several years later, I had the privilege of working with my dear friends SARK (Susan Ariel Rainbow Kennedy) and

Dr. John Waddell, who use "Inner Wise Self" terminology to describe that aspect of yourself that is consistently loving, supportive, and wise. Their interpretation adds to the joy and unconditional acceptance that comes with SELF love.

I incorporated all of these concepts into my personal definition of SELF. I merged the ideas of IFS with those of the Chopra Center, Inner Wise Self, and my own personal belief system (along with the teachings of many other mentors and guides I've had along the way) to come up with my concept of being "in SELF" in Compassionate Communication and Compassionate Mediation. I am deeply grateful to all of those whose wisdom and inspiration contributed to this work. You have all helped me professionally and personally in countless ways.

After 20 years of marriage, I realized that my marriage was not to last. I truly wanted to find a different way to end a relationship that I thought I'd be in until I died. I still loved my husband, but irreconcilable differences had made our continued marriage impossible. My divorce and my work evolved into an effort to bring those qualities of calm, clarity, courage, confidence and compassion to separation and divorce.

I tried to communicate from SELF as much as I could in my own life, at the same time I was teaching the tools to thousands of men and women who came to see me as clients. I saw that even if only one person in a relationship chooses to learn the skills of Compassionate Communication and Compassionate Mediation, the future of conflict resolution and separation and divorce can all become more SELF-led.

I want to share what I've learned so that you and your partner can discover what you each want to do moving forward. As you practice the skills of Compassionate Mediation, you will gain knowledge and tools to strengthen and transform your union, no matter what form it takes in the future.

To My Editors

Deepest gratitude to my dear cousin, Leonard Sherp, and my good friend, CJ Schepers. I value their dedicated guidance and expertise, which helped me create this book for you.

And special thanks to my esteemed mentor and colleague, davidji, for his beautiful foreword.

I send my love and heartfelt appreciation to you all.

Introduction

"Love and compassion are necessities, not luxuries. Without them humanity cannot survive. I truly believe that compassion provides the basis of human survival."
—Tenzin Gyatso, the XIVth Dalai Lama

"Should I Stay or Should I Go?"

How many times have you asked yourself this question—over how many days, weeks, months, years, even decades? Do you feel like your relationship is difficult and don't know how to change it? Have you had marriage counseling that didn't work? Are you too "checked out" to try again?

Have you ever considered the possibility of divorce, but were not sure what to do next? Are you too scared to even discuss it? Maybe you're reluctant to talk with an attorney because that would make the situation "real." Or perhaps you've threatened to leave the union for so long now that your partner doesn't believe you anymore.

Right now, you may be suffering in silence or engaged in all-out battle. Or you might be separated from your partner and each trying to live your own lives without a clear sense of direction for your relationship. But it doesn't have to stay that way.

When a marriage is in crisis, you suffer from unmet expectations, dashed hopes, stored resentments, quiet desperation or even overt war. You may have created an "impenetrable wall" around your heart as a way to "manage your pain" and protect yourself from more hurt and disappointment. You may have erected "filters" through which you see your partner, clouded with judgment or blame for what she/he did or didn't do. ("She *always* does this, he *never* does that.")

If you feel you've reached the end of your rope—that you can't go on this way any longer, that you're at a crossroads and don't know which way to turn next—before you take a step in any direction, it's time to come home to your SELF.

My Heart Goes Out to You

You may be reading this book because you are struggling with indecision, trying to decide what to do about your relationship, your family, and your future. You're likely experiencing many emotions—from sadness, anger, hurt and betrayal, to frustration, guilt, confusion, and a sense of being overwhelmed. I know this is an extremely difficult time because I've been there myself.

My Story

I was once where you are now, and it's a painful, lonely place. I discussed my situation with friends, family members, therapists, and loved ones. Ultimately, however, no one could make my decision for me. There were moments I was clear and determined, but more often, I was trapped in a state of limbo, unable to leave but unhappy in the marriage. Because I have experienced divorce firsthand, I have much to share about what to do—and what not to do.

I was happily married to my college sweetheart, but after twenty years together, we were looking at the possibility of a divorce. I worried about my children, my family, our future. I loved my husband, but we had reached an impasse about what was important to each of us moving forward in our lives. I was unsure what was the right thing to do, and in my uncertainty, I stayed stuck.

For years, I asked myself, *"Should I stay or should I go?"* In the decade it finally took me to decide, I took the pain of my own failings and missteps and turned them into lessons learned and methods developed that are now helping others succeed.

As I struggled with my own marriage and emotions, I returned to school to study psychotherapy, earning my second graduate degree and becoming a licensed clinical professional counselor, as well as a mediator and attorney. *Surely*, I thought, *as a lawyer, mediator, and therapist, I could get us through our divorce as smoothly and painlessly as possible.* But trying to mediate your own divorce is like trying to deliver your own baby. It may be remotely possible, but ultimately, it's much too difficult.

I thought that by staying together, our family was "intact." But we didn't have the tools to have all the conversations we needed to decide together the best road for each of us and our children. Although we stay married for a long time, there were years of pain, fear and indecision that affected us all.

I believed I was being helpful to my children. I thought I was keeping both parents available, even though we were separated. I finally realized that my ambivalence, vacillation, and procrastination created more harm than good. I often felt lost, alone, and didn't know what I needed to do next.

There Has to Be a Better Way

Years later, when I was sitting in a courtroom for a pre-trial hearing, with my estranged husband on one side and me on the other, I looked into my heart and I figured there had to be a better way. I watched the man who had been by my side at the birth of our two beautiful daughters, the guy who had been my best friend for over twenty years. His gaze avoided mine as we both sat on opposite sides of the room, feeling hurt, angry, afraid of the whole process we were in, and unable to re-connect. It was my worst nightmare come to life. Our marriage was ending, but did it have to end *this way*?

There *has* to be a better way to get divorced, I told myself. There *has* to be a better way to disconnect from someone you once promised to love forever. I wasn't sure how to make it better for myself, but I knew I wanted to help other people avoid the pain we were both feeling.

For most of my life, I have tried to see a divine plan in the experiences that I have been given. For over 30 years, I have tried to live a more spiritually based life instead of an "ego-based" life. When my ego takes the lead, as a way to manage the fear and uncertainty of the present or future, I have a need to control and judge and have my mind create expectations from my self (small 's'). In my attempt to lead a "spiritually based life," I do my best to communicate from my heart (where I connect with my higher SELF) as I stay open to what the Universe (or God) has planned for me.

I like the scholar and author Brené Brown's description of spirituality. She said, *"Spirituality is recognizing and celebrating that we are all inextricably connected to each other by a power greater than all of us, and that our connection to that power and to one another is grounded in love and compassion. Practicing spirituality brings a sense of perspective, meaning, and purpose to our lives."*

My own personal belief system is foundational for how I got to where I am. You do not have to have any of these beliefs to benefit from the tools I've developed for Compassionate Mediation®. Compassionate Mediation is based on the concepts of Compassionate Communication—or SELF-leadership—along with informed and empowered choices.

Whatever your individual belief system, I hope you will take what you can from this book and use it to help yourself heal and transform your relationship and your family. I know that this process has helped thousands of men and women, and I believe it can offer you some tools to use in your life now.

I agree with the message of Debbie Ford, who wrote in her book, *Spiritual Divorce*, *"Divorce can be a spiritual wake up call during which we have an opportunity to explore our inner world and begin the process of becoming intimate with our entire self—divorce brings us back into the presence of our highest self and heals the split between our ego and our soul."*

After years of working with individuals and couples who were considering or going through a divorce, I created the process of Compassionate Mediation to help you bring your highest and best SELF to your current situation. Then you can make your decision from a more expanded and loving state of awareness.

You will become more *conscious* of your own thoughts and behaviors. You will learn the skill of Compassionate Communication, in which you drop down from that egoic, judgmental, blaming *mind* and you drop into your *heart*, which is filled with love and compassion. The secret to *receiving* more compassion is learning how to *be* more compassionate. To paraphrase Gandhi, *"Be the change you wish to see in your relationship."* It starts with compassion for yourself, and then extending your compassion to your partner. You can then safely discuss your feelings, expectations, hopes, dreams, and possibilities as you create something new and better together.

Sometimes Compassionate Mediation is something only you will learn because your partner may not want to participate. The process of Compassionate Mediation allows you to accept your circumstances with peace, with forgiveness, with understanding and compassion.

I never wanted my divorce to create the pain and suffering that I had witnessed others endure. I procrastinated for years, as I learned to mediate, meditate, journal, do yoga, talk, get therapy, write, cry, pray and offer counsel to others. I realized in working with my clients that I had developed a peaceful and respectful process that would ultimately be a healing experience as two individuals who once loved each other and created a family together, learned how to respectfully go their separate ways. I wanted to do this for my husband and myself, but especially for our two daughters, who were 8 and 12 when we separated.

You Can Help Your Children

The world needs to be a safer place for marriage and divorce. Children should be shielded from the shrapnel of their parents' animosity. Compassionate Mediation offers a new paradigm for couples at a crossroads.

The more experience I have, the more compassion I have for the profound sadness and fear underneath my clients' resentments or rage. No matter how far apart a couple can become emotionally and physically, their children are caught in the middle and continue to feel the strife.

I believe families need not be "broken," but can be peacefully and respectfully "re-structured."

It's Never Too Late

Often there is one member of a couple who feels it's "too late" to save the relationship. **However, if just one of you will learn a new way to communicate, miracles can happen and a new and better union can emerge.**

I often tell my clients: *"This current marriage is 'over.' It's not about 'fixing' or 'saving' it or 'settling' for what you have. You can create a new and better relationship that is based on who you both are now, what's important to you, and what you are willing to give to the other of what you each want and need."*

Your children will only have one biological mother and father, no matter how many other partners are introduced into their lives. Children of all ages seek on some level to have a "happy family." If you can't find a way to live with the other parent, you can find a way to connect or disconnect with civility, courtesy, and even kindness. Healing can happen, and it starts with you.

Often imagining what the end of your relationship would look like will motivate you and your spouse to try to *heal* your relationship instead of *leaving* it. If you're feeling stuck or unsure about your relationship, or unable to communicate effectively, you *can* create a more peaceful and respectful connection with Compassionate Mediation. You will be able to make changes *before* divorce becomes your only option.

You will have a safe forum to talk about everything that has caused you pain or conflict. The conversations will cover all areas of contention or impasse—money, parenting, extended family, work, responsibilities, and even sex. You will be able to discuss everything in a whole new way. Whenever you communicate with more confidence, clarity and compassion, it is possible to create a new, enriching relationship with your partner. Or you can make a peaceful, *conscious* decision to separate or divorce.

You'll give yourself the necessary time it takes to focus respectfully and honestly on potential, positive outcomes rather than making a unilateral or irreversible decision to end your marriage. At the same time, however, the sooner you begin the process of Compassionate Mediation, the sooner you'll begin to make the changes that will heal your family, no matter what form that family takes in the future.

Love is the Answer—and It Starts with Loving Your SELF

Compassionate Mediation is an opportunity to talk about everything that has been a problem, and a chance to create a new marriage to the person you're living with now.

You begin to love yourself enough to do the work you need to heal the burdens from the past. You learn how to let go of any limiting beliefs that keep you from being open to new possibilities. You connect to your heart, your higher SELF, your witnessing awareness and your wisdom, and then you bring *that* energy back into your relationship. This book will give you the tools to put these ideals into practice, including links to my website for more support and a deeper dive into your own personal healing and transformation.

Looking at an ending can help create a new beginning. Compassionate Mediation is a short-term process that helps you bring your best SELF to your relationship so that you can co-create a new and better relationship—no matter what form it takes.

You can take the time you need to learn more about Compassionate Communication, Compassionate Relationships, and Compassionate Mediation. You will see that if you're going to make the decision to get divorced, you can create a compassionate and SELF-Led Divorce®, in which you're communicating from your highest and best SELF for the benefit of all concerned.

The Stress of Uncertainty

Divorce is one of life's major stressors, but perhaps "wondering if you should get a divorce" can sometimes be more stressful than actually making a decision and moving forward. When you finally decide whether to stay or go, you can confidently move in that one direction. When you are not sure what you want to do, life becomes a series of vastly different possibilities, each with its own set of fears and concerns.

You might wonder, **"What if I stay and it never gets any better?"** You then project a lifetime where you are stuck in a relationship that doesn't meet your needs and brings out the worst version of your self.

Perhaps you worry, **"What if I leave and I'm all alone and broke and without my children?"** You begin to picture all the horrors that are possible, and turn around and vacillate some more. The stress of indecision and procrastination, feeling stuck and overwhelmed is often worse than making a choice. Author Anais Nin has said, *"And the day came when the risk to remain tight in a bud was more painful than the risk it took to blossom."* You have your own choice to make. You can stay where you are or you can explore the possibilities of change.

The constant uncertainty, vacillation, and ambivalence make it hard for you to be present in a calm and peaceful way. You are constantly worrying about your future, concentrating on what is wrong with the present, and ruminating about the pain from the past. All of that behavior increases the feelings of stress that affect your emotional, psychological and physical health. Divorce is almost as stressful as the death of a loved one. It is a different kind of death—the death of a relationship, the death of a marriage, and often the most difficult, the death of a dream.

Explore All Your Options

Compassionate Mediation is a process that helps you either add *passion* to your marriage or *compassion* to your divorce. You don't have to spend years "on the fence" in an unhappy or dysfunctional relationship. You can learn how to speak your truth courageously and set healthy boundaries confidently. You will discover what you truly want and need, believe that you deserve to be happy and fulfilled, and learn how to ask respectfully, receive graciously, and share your gratitude. You will begin to experience more love in your life, even if it means you give it to yourself.

You will learn how to become more empathetic and considerate—first for yourself, and then your partner. You will know how to ask for and get your needs met and forgive yourself and each other. You will remember how to be grateful again for what you do share, and learn how to reflect the attention, affection, appreciation, and acceptance you both desire—no matter the outcome.

You will learn that it's not always *what* you say but *how* you say it. You will experience the healing power of "thank you" and "I'm sorry." You will safely explore all your options to re-structure your family peacefully and respectfully.

Remember Who You Truly Are

The French philosopher Teilhard de Chardin said, *"We are not human beings having a spiritual experience. We are spiritual beings having a human experience."* You can always tune in to who you truly are, underneath your thoughts, feelings, and past experiences. You can connect with what I believe is your divine spiritual nature in the midst of your human experiences. You become more conscious, aware, mindful—in other words, more "SELF-led." You learn how to choose your responses, your behavior, and your future decisions from your highest and best SELF. Becoming more conscious and SELF-led in your relationship allows you to focus on the higher good for all concerned, and then relate compassionately to heal and transform the dynamics between you and your partner.

In her new book of the same title, Katherine Woodard has described her process of "Conscious Uncoupling" as a loving way to end a marriage. When you are in SELF, you can also choose to *consciously couple* in a way that leads to more intimacy, passion, connection and fun. You will feel more balanced, peaceful, openhearted, open-minded, and present. This book will help you bring your best SELF into all your relationships.

How to Use This Book

I've divided the book into the following sections. Reading them in order gives you a step-by-step guide, but you can go to any section that calls to you first. There are questions for you in many chapters, and the more you answer them, the more inner guidance you will receive.

I suggest that you start a new journal if you'd like, and allow yourself to start the next chapter of your life now as you take the steps to confidently, courageously and calmly explore all of your possibilities.

SECTION ONE: Compassionate Communication Begins with You

Compassionate Mediation begins with learning the skill of Compassionate Communication. Connecting to your best SELF—as you let go of limiting beliefs, heal burdens from your past, and relate from your heart—is the foundation for Compassionate Relationships, Compassionate Mediation, and Compassionate or SELF-Led Divorce®.

As you become more compassionate with your SELF, you will become more willing and able to extend that compassion to others. Your new way of communicating will be evident in the speech you use, your tone of voice, and how you respond. You can unburden your pain from the past, stay "in the now", and relate in a non-blaming or non-judgmental manner.

Compassionate Communication is a conscious, higher-SELF directed way of relating to others that invites empathy and understanding. Instead of building "walls" around your heart, you create healthy boundaries. You begin to recognize the influence of your Family of Origin and take care of your

"Inner Child," which may be holding onto pain from your past. You learn a new way to communicate that peacefully resolves conflict as you heal wounds from the past and stay present to create a better future.

SECTION TWO: Compassionate Mediation to Become Your Own Best Advocate

You can create a new and better relationship, no matter what form it ultimately takes. You get clear on what is important to you, learn that you deserve to be happy, get confident to ask for what you want, become willing to receive, and stay grateful for all you already share. You do your own healing first. Then you will have the tools to create a new relationship with your partner or on your own.

Your relationship begins to change as you do. You will educate and empower yourself with legal and financial information. It is often these detailed conversations that instill a desire to try harder to heal the pain from the past, forgive yourself and your partner, and create a new and better marriage together. When you become fully informed of the financial reality of your current situation, coupled with newfound empathy for the feelings of your partner, you can make changes that can immediately impact your relationship in a positive way.

However, if your ultimate decision is to get a divorce, Compassionate Mediation will provide the framework for a peaceful and respectful SELF-Led Divorce.

SECTION THREE: Reduce Your Stress with Exquisite SELF-Care

Stress is often due to not getting your needs met, and when there is conflict or disharmony in your relationship, stress is always present. You can lower your stress, by tuning into your SELF with breathing, yoga, meditation, and other modalities. You will also be guided on how to let go of limiting beliefs and heal burdens from your past so that you can feel more balance, peace, and joy. You may believe that "when you make a decision, you'll feel better." But the opposite is true. When you *feel better*, you'll be able to make the right decision for yourself and your family.

SECTION FOUR: Make Decisions from Your Highest SELF

Will you end up with a new Compassionate Relationship or a peaceful and compassionate SELF-Led Divorce? As you practice Compassionate Communication and discuss your options through Compassionate Mediation, you and your partner can each bring your best SELF into a new and improved *passionate* relationship. Learning to show compassion rather than judgment makes deeper and connection possible. Your relationships with others will also improve. You will learn how to talk with your children, family and friends as you instill a message of cooperation and friendship to be shared by all.

You may realize that you and your partner have each done the best you knew how to do, that you're grateful for all that you've shared, and yet you realize it's time to go your separate ways. You can then consider a divorce that is created from your highest and best SELF. You can heal from the past and move forward with forgiveness, friendship, and freedom.

SECTION FIVE: Compassion for All

You offer compassion to your children, your parents, your friends, co-workers, and your extended family. You will become more patient with the *process* of counseling, mediation, separation and/or divorce, so that you can make your decisions from a place of SELF-leadership and higher consciousness. You will also learn how to be more compassionate with new partners, step-families and everyone touched by your present and future decisions. Your own inner peace is one step in the direction of family peace. Your higher SELF brings you to new heights of consciousness, connection, and compassion for yourself and others.

If couples put as much energy into learning how to communicate with compassion as they have to put into getting a divorce, profound changes can occur within them and between them.

I'm Here to Help

I hope that you will use this book as you would the support of a friend, one who has been there and one who cares. If you are feeling conflicted, uncertain, scared, or alone, take some time to breathe and relax. Life will get better. You will learn a safe way to have those discussions you've been avoiding. Compassionate Mediation embraces spiritual wisdom from many teachers to create a new paradigm for communication. You can *transform your relationship* instead of *dissolving your marriage.*

While we routinely recognize the pain and suffering from wars and illnesses, I wonder how many other casualties can be attributed to the fall of a family. How many innocent bystanders are harmed by the decision of two people to terminate a marriage? How many generations pay the price of familial conflict?

I know there is a better way. I watch my clients create it. I hope you can change your relationship struggles into an experience that enriches your family rather than continuing on the current pathways that may be destroying it. Should you stay or go? Only you have that answer. Compassionate Mediation can show you how to find it.

I offer you my experience and my knowledge to coach you as you move forward from wherever you are now to wherever you're hoping to be. I'm here to help in any way I can. From my heart to yours, I'm sending a great deal of love and support.

SECTION ONE
Compassionate Communication Begins with You

Chapter 1
Connect to Your Highest and Best SELF

"Love is the great miracle cure.
Loving ourselves works miracles in our lives."
—Louise L. Hay, Author

Would You Like to Have More Love and Happiness?

You *can* begin to add more peace, love and joy to all of your relationships—starting now. The secret is learning how to communicate with compassion—first for yourself, and then for others.

How Compassionate Are You Being with Your SELF?

If you could totally and completely accept yourself, love yourself, and forgive yourself for any choice you've made or not made up until this point, would you do it? Would you:

- Show yourself the same care and consideration you give to others?

- Applaud yourself for all that you have accomplished?

- Understand you've done the best you knew how to do?

- Believe you are exactly where you need to be at this point in time?

3

I hope you answered "yes" to at least one of these questions. Too often you are your own worst critic with those "woulda, coulda, shoulda" critical refrains playing in your head. As you practice Compassionate Communication, you will learn how to be more caring and compassionate with yourself and then you will do the same with your partner. He or she will eventually respond the same way. If they don't begin to show you more love and compassion, you may have some decisions to make at a later date. If you have to make some difficult choices in the future, you will know that you did everything that you could do to first communicate from your highest and best SELF.

The way you relate to your partner is often a mirror image of how you relate to your SELF. If you took a picture of your relationship right now, what would you see? Would you:

- See love and respect?

- Feel kindness and generosity?

- Experience understanding and forgiveness?

- Receive gratitude and compassion?

Once again, I hope you answered "yes," but you probably didn't—which is why you're reading this book. And if I asked you to apply those same questions to how you relate to your SELF, you might also reply in the negative. However, as you learn how to improve your love and care for your SELF, you will see all of your relationships heal and transform. You will bring a new energy of calm, compassionate communication to create a new and better interaction with your partner.

In your version of a "perfect world," it might seem wonderful to imagine your partner changing to meet your needs. That may actually happen, but you must first identify and articulate what those needs are. Usually couples resort to a constant replay of all their complaints and judgments, rather than learning how to share their feelings, desires, hopes and dreams. Compassionate Communication is the road back to each other, no matter what choices you make in the future.

You've had those moments when you feel, calm, clear and compassionate—moments when you're free of judgment or anger toward others, and simply respond from your heart, your higher SELF. Think about those times when you just *knew* you were seeing the world from a *higher perspective*. You didn't have to force it. It just happened.

This chapter is all about guiding you back to your SELF. When you are "in SELF," answers to your questions will come to you with ease. You won't have to agonize about which direction to pursue. You will be led by that inner wisdom which is always available when you quiet your mind enough to hear it.

Compassionate Communication allows you to connect to your best SELF, let go of limiting beliefs, unburden pain from the past, and relate from your heart.

SELF and "Parts"

Many terms are used to describe our most centered, compassionate, and spiritual nature: for example, *true self, inner wisdom, higher self, Soul, Spirit, Universe, Oneness, source energy, Buddha nature, Brahman, Inner Wise Self, Inner Wisdom, Inner Pilot Light, higher consciousness,* etc. Regardless of your belief systems, and in the interest of laying common ground and language between us, I will call this best, most loving, wisest part of us—the **SELF** (all capital letters).

In their new book, *Reform Your Inner Mean Girl: 7 Steps to Stop Bullying Yourself and Start Loving Yourself,* Amy Ahlers and Christine Arylo describe "Inner Wisdom, " what I call "higher SELF" as *"The loving presence that loves you unconditionally and as a result can offer compassion and care to you no matter what. This wise, inner guidance system knows exactly what direction will lead to your highest good, and so can tell you the best course of action to take. It's the honest, give-it-to-me straight voice that, like a trusted friend, tells you the truth even when it's hard to hear—but always tells you with compassion and without judgment."*

Whenever you operate from SELF, you're calmer, clearer, and more compassionate. You speak with greater confidence and courage, as you stay connected to your deep, inner knowing. You're no longer making decisions from old, reactive "Parts" of you that are scared, walled up, judgmental, angry, or retaliatory. You're able to stay in the present moment and co-create a relationship that considers *everyone's* needs, starting with your own.

Whenever you're in SELF you can speak *for* your Parts instead of *from* your Parts. Then you communicate with honesty, empathy, and clarity.

My dear friend and mentor SARK describes your "Inner Wise Self" which *"is and always will be your unconditional source of love. No matter how thoughtful and attentive, no person can ever give you the ongoing unconditional love that you have from your Inner Wise Self. The more you feel that self-love, the more you are able to be in a relationship as a strong, independent partner."*

Some Similar Terms for "SELF"

Awareness

Authentic Self

Brahman

Buddha Nature

Christ Consciousness

Compassion

Compassionate
    Communication

Consciousness

Divine

Divine Nature

Divine Presence

Divinity

Energy

Father

God

Goddess

Heart

Higher Consciousness

Higher Self

Holy Spirit

Inner Wise Self

Inner Pilot Light

Mother

Nature

Oneness

Pure Positive Energy

SELF

Soul

Spark

Spirit

True Self

Universe

Please add your own terms

Unfortunately, most of us find it difficult to operate consistently in SELF-mode. More often, we've learned how to relate from our "Parts." The way back to "SELF" is to first know, understand, and love our Parts.

You first said, "I do," with the thought of staying married forever, and now you and your partner have developed some bad habits in your method of communication. Many individuals are afraid to share their honest feelings and unmet needs with their partner, so they suffer in silence, act out in rage, or secretly disconnect and find another partner with whom to have an affair. You might withdraw when you're angry or get angry when you're sad. You might be looking at your partner with a "filter" of judgment or blame from some unresolved issues from your past together. Perhaps you have built a "wall around your heart" to keep yourself from feeling too close or too vulnerable because you don't want to be hurt again.

Problems in relationships are rarely about *what* you are saying, but *how* you are saying it. Parts often carry a negative energy or tone. Whenever you speak from SELF, you create more acceptance, attention, appreciation, and affection for each other.

Your SELF in Compassionate Mediation

Compassionate Communication and Compassionate Mediation follow many principles of Internal Family Systems Therapy (IFS). As defined on the IFS website, www.selfleadership.org, *"IFS helps you understand the suffering of your wounded, exiled parts (or your "inner child") and also to appreciate the good intentions of the protective Manager parts. IFS provides a clear approach to transforming and healing all Parts by reconnecting them to the powerful core Self that exists in each of us."*

I have created my own introduction to the concept of SELF and Parts for my clients, which follows. (I offer it with deep gratitude to Dick Schwartz and all my IFS colleagues who can be found at *www.selfleadership.org*.)

Introduction to SELF and Parts

"I believe we all have a healthy SELF, with a capital 'S" and when we're "in SELF," we are calm, clear, and compassionate. You know those moments: they are usually just moments, and the rest of the time we're in our "Parts," and I call those groups of parts Exiles, Managers and Extremes."

Exiles are the Parts we have hidden (often since childhood) when our needs were not getting met. Whenever we were sad, scared, hurt, vulnerable, we didn't want to feel that way, so we pushed those uncomfortable feelings aside. Some of us exiled our anger, too, because it wasn't safe (or acceptable) to express it. Exiles often wonder, "What about me? Who's going to love and care for me the way I need?"

Managers are the protective Parts that get formed to help us cope with the feelings from those Exiles. Some of us learned how to be nice, pleasing, or care-taking. Others became blaming, judgmental, or angry. There are numerous ways to manage our exiled pain, sadness, fear, and anger. In fact, many of us have learned to play a Manager Part, which looks like a "Pseudo-Self," in which we appear calm on the surface, but underneath still feel sad, hurt, fearful, or angry.

But the Managers can only protect us for so long. Whenever the pain of those Exiles can't be "managed," other Parts appear, the **Extremes**, which numb us or help us escape. Extremes often show up

11

as addictions—to food, alcohol, drugs, work, television, and more. We may keep ourselves too busy, raise emotional walls, wallow in depression, or become enraged. Sometimes, we have an affair or get divorced without even thinking of the repercussions.

You and your partner are each your own castle. While the Exiles are hanging out in the dungeon, afraid to be seen, the Managers are standing guard ready to defend against an attack. Then as soon as someone or something feels too threatening, the Extremes take over. The only way for safety to be happen is for SELF to be present, and my job is to help you get to SELF."

Some of My Parts

My father was a lovable undiagnosed manic-depressive who was one of the funniest men I've ever met. However, he was also prone to fits of rage. I learned at a young age that anger was scary, and I *exiled* those parts of me that could have used my anger to set healthy boundaries in the future. I *managed* by becoming a codependent pleaser—trying to be nice and make everyone happy—and operating from a place of wanting to be liked. When I became exhausted trying to please everyone and denying my feelings and needs, I would over-indulge in chocolate, work, and too many reruns of television shows. My other *Extreme* reactions included an eating disorder and a chronic health problem.

My father's behavior caused me to be afraid of anger, eventually even my own. When my boundaries felt violated, I would move the boundaries rather than share my feelings and assert my rights. During the separation from my husband, I was afraid to confront issues and procrastinated taking positive actions. Instead of making a call to my estranged husband to discuss our issues, I would go eat chocolate and stay up late at night watching television. I was numbing myself rather than confronting the decisions that needed to be made. My behavior was confusing and unfair to both of us. We were each doing the best we could do at that time, but I wish we could have done it better.

As I studied Internal Family Systems Therapy and did my own healing work, I learned how to ask my Managing Parts to relax and to trust me as I communicated from my SELF about all my exiled feelings, wants, and needs. I learned how to remind my Inner Child that I was no longer powerless as I had been when I was young. I assured her that I could protect her from other people's anger, and that she would be safe with me forevermore. It took time to prove it to myself, but the more I took positive action, the better I felt.

When I was "in SELF," I tried to be as compassionate as I could with my husband, who also had his own fears, pain, and anger. As I did my own work to relate more from SELF than from my Parts, our relationship changed. I became willing to speak my truth with courage and confidence. I learned how to stop managing my fears, and instead began to share my feelings. I was no longer limited by the outdated beliefs of my Managing Parts (that used to believe anger was not safe and I always had to be "nice"), and I made new choices that were more SELF-led. My honesty led to some conflict, but we eventually resolved our differences rather than spending more years in limbo.

You and your partner both might be stuck in various Parts that keep replicating the same dynamics of your past, which leads you to believe that divorce is the only way out. Once *even one of you* learns to access your higher SELF, your relationship will begin to transform. You still may choose to separate or divorce, but the process can be more peaceful and respectful than your current relationship. You can become more *conscious* and *aware* of what is happening between you, rather than just unconsciously reacting to the various Parts of each other.

In her book, *Guilt is the Teacher, Love is the Answer,* Joan Boryshenko said, *"Rather than thinking in terms of good and bad, it is more helpful to think in terms of conscious and unconscious, aware and unaware."* When you are "in SELF," you are practicing "witnessing awareness" of the behaviors of your Parts and your partner's Parts. You can *notice* what is happening between you and then make *conscious* choices to respond in ways that foster better communication.

When I notice anger now, I can also be aware of the wounded Inner Child who is struggling to get his needs met, and I can send compassion to that Inner Child; at the same time, I set a boundary with the angry Part that may seem to be attacking me.

You Can Make a Difference: Do Your Own Work First

It's important that you and your partner each do your *own work,* but if only one of you is willing, the dynamics of your relationship can still change. When SELF is present (even if it just comes from you), the relationship improves immediately. You will *understand* your own unique Parts in order to heal the past and connect to your spiritual source—whatever that means to you. The more you practice acceptance, forgiveness, humility, responsibility, compassion, and non-judgment, the more liberating life becomes—not only for yourself, but everyone around you.

The following page is my "Chart of SELF and Parts" that I show to all my clients. There are many more Parts, to offer you a general idea.

SELF

CALM, CLEAR, COMPASSIONATE, COURAGEOUS, CONFIDENT, CURIOUS, CREATIVE, CONNECTED, GRATEFUL

PARTS

EXILES	MANAGERS	EXTREME
Hurt	*Angry	Addictions
Sad	Caretaking	Affairs
Scared	Controlling	Depression
Vulnerable	Critical	Drinking
	Distant	Drug Use
(Angry)	Judgmental	Eating
	Nice	Gambling
	Perfectionistic	*Rage
	Sarcastic	Shopping
		Walls
"WHAT ABOUT ME?	*"PSEUDO-SELF"*	*"WAYS TO NUMB"*
Inner Child	*Mind/Ego*	*Reactive*

(*Some people Exile their anger, others use it as a Manager, and many others use it as an Extreme Part as rage. The Exiles represent some of the repressed feelings of your "Inner Child," whereas the Managers are more related to how you show yourself to the world. Extreme parts are very reactive as a way to numb from the feelings of the Exiles when the Managers can't contain them.)

For a video of my introduction to SELF and PARTS, please go to LindaKroll.com/book-resources

You Can Ask Your SELF:

- What could this relationship become if *I* changed in it?
- What can I do to bring my best SELF to my relationship?
- Can I forgive myself and my partner?
- How can I be more calm, clear, courageous, confident, compassionate?
- How can I stop *reacting* and start *responding* from my highest and best SELF?
- What would happen if I took down the *walls* I have built around my heart?
- What if I could change the *filters* through which I judge my partner?
- What if we could do a "start over" and create something new that would meet both of our needs?
- What if I could learn to look at the events that bothered me from a higher state of consciousness, where I could be the calm in the middle of the storm and see what I was to learn, rather than control?
- What if I could allow myself to be more authentic and empathic?
- What if?
- And if so, then how?

As you tune into your highest and best SELF, the answers will begin to appear.

Ways to "Get to SELF"
To Receive Your Inner Guidance

Angels
Art
Ask for it
Body Scan
Breathe
Chakra Balancing
Channeling
Children
Chi gong
Collage Making
Coloring
Cooking
Connecting
Dance
Deep Breathing
Drawing
Dreams
Drumming
Flowers
Focusing
Gardening
Guided Imagery
Hobbies
Intuition

Journaling
Knowing Place
Labyrinth
Laughter
Letting Go
Listening
Loving
Mandala
Mantra
Massage
Meditation
Miracles
Movement
Music
Nature
Nia
Painting
Parts
   (sending love)
Pause
Pets
Prayer
Private Place
Reiki

Running
Silence
Singing
Sleeping
Slowing Down
Solitude
Space
Sports
Stars
Surrender
Sweat Lodge
Synchronicity
Swimming
Tai Chi
Talking
Quiet Mind/Body
Walking
Workshops
Writing
Yoga

Please add your own terms

The Power of SELF-Leadership

Some of my clients ask me, *"Why should I have to do any more work? I was always the only one who cared enough to try harder!"*

When you do your own work to "get to SELF," you will bring the best version of who you are—and how you can be—back to your relationship. You will no longer be reacting in old patterns that have co-created your current situation. Take a moment and get a new perspective on your own Parts, to help you heal and transform your relationship.

The work you do is ultimately for your own personal growth. With or without your (former) partner present, you can explore the origins of your own pain and anger, and learn how to communicate your needs in words that don't sound blaming or judgmental. You can learn how to talk about your sadness and your fears, *even if the end result is a decision to leave your marriage.*

When there is an intense emotional impasse, you can fall into a pattern of fight-flight—where sarcasm or withdrawal is your weapon of choice—or frozen suspended animation, where you feel too immobilized to move in any direction, so you stay stuck in limbo, indecisive and fearful.

It's no secret that half of all first marriages end in divorce. But it may be surprising to learn that the failure rates for second and third marriages get even worse: 67 and 73 percent, respectively, according to a 2012 article in *Psychology Today,* "The High Failure Rate of Second and Third Marriages."

But what about the statistics on married people who are "thinking" about divorce? Researchers estimate that 1 in 3 divorced couples try to reconcile later. Often, one or both partners believe that divorce is the only way out of the pain. However, a significant number of divorced individuals— *about half*—says they wished they or their spouse had tried harder to save the marriage. The problem is that they don't know how.

In other words, divorce is all too common, and there's a lot of regret out there. If you are at a crossroads in your marriage, you can take the time to communicate with compassion and create something new. Instead of *"Should I stay or should I go?"* the question you can ask yourself *is "How can I be my best SELF in this relationship and see what comes next?"* You can create either a deeper, richer, and happier union, or a peaceful and respectful Compassionate SELF-led Divorce.

Even if your partner doesn't want to read this book, your connection together can still change. All it takes is one person, one SELF, to make a shift.

Guided Meditation to Access SELF

As you think about all the problems in your relationship, you can begin to notice your physical responses to your thoughts. I offer the following guided meditation to get a "felt sense" of what being "in SELF" feels like. I offer it in my first session with deep gratitude to Richard Schwartz, who first guided me "up the mountain."

You can read it below, or go to my website to listen to the audio version at LindaKroll.com/book-resources.

SELF "Up the Mountain" Meditation

Take a deep breath, a full breath all the way into your abdomen, and just release it with a sigh. Take another one, down to your belly, and release. One more, and then let your breath return to its normal pattern.

As your feet touch the ground, imagine they are growing roots to the center of the Earth. Those roots grow wider and deeper until you begin to feel very firmly rooted or planted or grounded, like a tree or a mountain, so that whatever happens around you isn't going to take you off your foundation.

You can allow the nurturing energy from the Earth to go up through your feet, calves, thighs, groin, lungs, chest, and into and around your heart, with all the feelings that are there.

23

Allow the energy to go up your throat, into your jaw, behind your eyes, to the crown of your head, and then out the crown of your head, all the way to the sky. You can then invite down from the sky, Heaven, Nature, the Universe, God, Higher Power—whatever is out there for you—invite down some energy that is very calm and very compassionate.

Then breathe even bigger than yourself, so that you can surround yourself with this calm, compassionate energy that is the energy of your SELF. Now gently focus that compassion inward. Scan your body, from the crown of your head to the soles of your feet, and just notice.

Notice where you feel tension and tightness. Notice your thoughts. Notice your feelings. And as you notice all these Parts, let these Parts notice YOU, being divinely supported, inspired and surrounded by this calm, compassionate energy of your SELF.

Now, for a moment, imagine yourself going through a doorway, into a beautiful scene in nature. The sun is shining, and the air is perfect, and you see before you a path, which you safely walk to the base of a mountain. What you are going to do now is to *separate* from your Parts, and go up "in SELF" as high up the mountain as you would like.

So ask any Parts that are angry, resentful, frustrated, blaming or judgmental if they will separate. Ask the Parts that are impatient for a change, if they will separate. Ask the Parts that are nervous, worried, anxious, scared if they will separate. Ask all the Parts that are sad, hurt, wounded, vulnerable, if they will separate, too. Ask any Part that is not *Peace* to separate, while you go up "in SELF" as high up the mountain as you would like, all the way to the top if you want.

Wherever you decide to stop on the mountain, just rest, and look at the view from up here. You may be aware of another Presence, you may not; either way is fine. And if you want, you can put your thumb and forefinger together to remember this place, to which you can return whenever you want.

In just a few moments, you are going to go back down the mountain to reclaim your Parts. But before you do, in your mind's eye, picture your partner at the top of their mountain, without all their Parts attached, and, as much as you can, send compassion in his/her direction.

Now in a moment, you will begin to go down the mountain and reclaim your Parts (even if there is a Part of you that doesn't want to reclaim them.) You will realize that when you give your own Parts the attention they need to unburden the pain from the past, they carry their own wisdom and light.

Now, taking back your Parts ever so gently, come back down the mountain, back down the path, back through the doorway, and back to this present moment.

Take Some Time to Reflect

If you want to take a moment, you can journal your experience of being "in SELF."

- Were you able to show compassion to yourself?
- What are the Parts you asked to stay at the base of the mountain?
- Which of your Parts were not willing to separate?
- How did it feel to *just rest* in SELF?
- When you looked at your partner without judgment or blame, did you feel more compassion?
- Did you wish you could stay at the *top of the mountain?*
- Were there any of your own Parts that you *didn't want to take back?*
- Would you like to learn how to maintain those feelings of being "in SELF?"

If you would like to live your life more often "in SELF", you start by understanding and appreciating your Parts. When you learn to show yourself compassion, you can extend more compassion to others. Compassion is like a boomerang. Send it out there and see how quickly it comes back to you!

Chapter 2
Understand and Love Your Parts

"If we learn to open our hearts, anyone, including the people who drive us crazy, can be our teacher."
—Pema Chodron, Buddhist Nun and Author

Different People, Different Couples, Same Parts

Every person who comes to see me has a different set of issues in a different type of relationship. The configurations are endless. But the Parts of all the players are the same. They all have their Exiles, protected by their Managers, who are all defended by their Extreme Parts.

As you learn to separate from your Parts and relate from SELF, you can transform or unburden the Parts of yourself that need healing. You will then have the necessary clarity to make decisions about the future of your relationship.

When you come from SELF, there is no rancor or ugliness. You can decide that you each have grown in different ways and may be better off if you go your separate paths. You can be grateful for what you have shared, wish each other well, and let go with love. It may seem impossible, but it is a very real opportunity to heal your issues—both intra-personally (inside yourself) and interpersonally (between you and your partner) before you go on to the rest of your lives.

Compassionate Communication allows you to connect to your spiritual source or SELF, unburden pain from the past, let go of limiting beliefs, and relate from your heart. In this chapter, you'll learn how to do that by remembering who you truly are and learning to love yourself.

You Were Born a Light

I believe we come into this world as pure light—innocent, free, unencumbered. From the moment we are conceived, our environment, even in the womb, affects us. After our tumultuous journey through the birth canal, we begin to experience events that shape our view of ourselves and the world.

No matter how good a job our parents try to do, we all suffer trauma of one kind or another. Each time we experience pain, fear, sadness, a "black cloth" covers that original light until we eventually forget it is there within us.

Unburdening the effects of those traumatic experiences—whether the trauma was one event or many sustained over time—enables us to regain our connection to our own Inner Light. Many of us seek people or substances or experiences outside ourselves to try to find the light that we have lost sight of within us.

As we remember to "see the Light within," we connect to our hearts and to our Source of connection, whatever we call that Source—Higher Power, God, Nature, the Universe, Christ, Buddha, or a Consciousness that transcends our individual mind or ego. I'm calling that connection, being "in SELF."

No matter how harshly you sometimes judge yourself, you are no worse (and no better) than anyone else. Once you truly accept all Parts of yourself, you can truly accept others. You may want to change some of your behaviors. You may regret some of your actions in the past and need to make amends.

You can change by setting your intention to make better choices in the future. You can learn from the experiences in the past and become a better version of yourself *because* of all your choices in the past.

When SELF-Leadership and gratitude replace resentments, a new relationship can begin.

SELF-Leadership is Important

If you are not "in SELF," but speaking from your Parts, you may...

- Feel like a victim (Exile) or an aggressor (Extreme)
- Act "nice" (Manager) but secretly be furious
- Feel unable to participate reasonably because you feel so overwhelmed, betrayed, retributive, fearful, or depressed
- Stay "crazy busy" to avoid feeling your feelings at all.

When you take the time to become SELF-led, you will...

- Make **calm** and **clear** decisions
- Be **compassionate** for the roller coaster of emotions you feel and also have compassion for the feelings and needs of your spouse
- Feel **confident** asking for want you want and need
- Stay **connected** and participatory with the process of mediation or divorce
- Be **courageous** in the face of challenge or adversity
- Remain **curious** about options and possibilities
- **Co-create** reasonable solutions and a positive future
- Stay **grateful** for all you have shared with your partner

Identify Your Parts and Your Partner's Parts

What are some of your behaviors that are causing conflict or pain? What do you do to upset your partner? What does your partner do to trigger you?

Notice how your body feels when you start thinking about being upset. We'll come back to this later, but it's important to always be aware of how you feel, not just listening to what you *think*.

What Does Your Partner Do That Upsets You?

Right now, think of all the complaints you have about your partner.

- *He never listens.*
- *She's never happy.*
- *He always criticizes me.*
- *She spends too much money.*
- *He's never home.*
- *She doesn't want to have sex.*
- *He is rude to my family.*
- *She always focuses on the kids and never on me.*
- Add your own judgment, complaints, and resentments.

Now notice what is happening in your body as you focus on all the negatives and what you don't like about your partner or your situation. You might notice tension in your body as you replay the last few years. Underneath the judgments you have about each other are your feelings of sadness that are going unacknowledged. Instead of focusing on what you don't have, you will learn to ask for what you do want, and change the energy between you. Once you both learn how to speak for your sadness and fears, and ask for what you truly want and need, walls can come down safely and anger and resentment subside.

What feelings do you "Exile?"

Is it hard to talk about your sadness, fear, or pain?

Do you avoid being angry or stuff your feelings

How do you "Manage" your life?

How do you define yourself?

Are Parts of you exhausted from being so "nice," avoiding conflict, unable to say "no?"

Do you find yourself often blaming or judging others?

What would people say about you?

What "Extreme" behaviors do you use to numb your feelings?

Any addictions?

Too much activity?

Any behaviors you would like to change but keep repeating?

A Client Example

Mark and Sheila came to see me to end their marriage. She was full of rage and complained that he walled her out and would never communicate with her. When she left the room, Mark told me how afraid he was of her anger. His silence was his way of protecting himself from what felt like verbal abuse. I encouraged him to share his feelings of fear, sadness, and vulnerability with her. After the process of Compassionate Mediation, Mark was able to show the depth of his emotions (through his tears), his wife finally saw that he did have feelings, and she began to soften her tone and ask for what she needed instead of criticizing him.

The issues that lead to the possibility of divorce may still come up in the process of mediation. Does one of you have a problem with rage, or drinking, or drug use? Has there been or is there still an affair in progress? Does one of you feel intimidated by the other and often capitulate in an effort to "keep the peace?"

What Do You Do that Upsets Your Partner?

What would your partner say are the reasons he or she may want to leave the relationship? How long has your partner complained about these issues? What has been your response in the past? Have you tried to accommodate his or her feelings or needs, or have you put up an emotional wall or barrier to keep from being hurt again? Do you have any desire or intention to make changes that would lead to a better relationship?

Is There Any Chance to Create a New Marriage?

Ask yourself if there is any chance to create a "new marriage" together. If you each could relate with more empathy and compassion, would that make a difference now? If you could forgive yourself and each other, would that matter? Do both of you truly want a divorce, or is one of you issuing an ultimatum to coerce the other party into marital counseling?

Are You Really "Done" With the Marriage or Just Very Hurt?

If you are very hurt, there may be a way to heal the pain and lead you to "time out" (a separation) or even a "new marriage" together. If you are willing to do your own healing work, you can heal the past and pave a new direction for the future.

Many couples come to see me *long after* their troubles began. Compassionate Communication gives an individual or couple the tools they need to understand their history and how it has affected their present circumstances.

You can begin to look at your partner with more *understanding*. You realize that each of you is doing and has done the best you knew how to do considering the level of your awareness at the time. This realization makes it easier for *forgiveness* to flow and for *gratitude* to take the place of resentment and acrimony.

Your Family of Origin

Your Family of Origin is the family to which you were born or in which you grew up. When you focus your attention on your Family of Origin, you may begin to notice patterns of behavior emerging. You become aware of what you have witnessed and learned, and also how it has affected your habitual reactions in response to distress.

This carries over to your relationships and your marriage. You can review your early experiences and what expectations you brought into your relationship. Your belief system was shaped when you were very young. You came into your marriage with certain expectations based on your early beliefs. You took on a series of roles and behaviors consistent with those thoughts. Now you are unhappy and changes need to be made—by both of you. The change can begin with you as you connect to the inner light of your SELF.

A recent client sent me this note:

"Linda, so much gratitude for you! I am so thankful to have had the opportunity to work with you and discover, recognize and pay attention to all of my parts of "SELF." During my session yesterday I thought of this reading that I wanted to share with you. When you asked me what my life would have been life had the family circumstances been different, it led me right to this writing. ...thank you for giving me permission and demonstrating your light to help liberate me."

The writing that she included was the beautiful quote from Marianne Williamson that reads:

"Our deepest fear is not that we are inadequate. Our deepest fear is that we are 'powerful beyond measure'. It is our light, not darkness, that most frightens us. We ask ourselves, who am I to be brilliant, gorgeous, talented, fabulous? Actually, who are you not to be. You are a child of God. Your playing small doesn't serve the world. There's nothing enlightened about shrinking so that other people won't feel insecure around you. You were born to manifest the glory of God that is within you. It's not just in some of us; it's in everyone and as we let our own light shine, we unconsciously give other people permission to do the same. As we are liberated from our own fear, our presence automatically liberates others."

You can remember the Light that you are, and shine that Light in your relationship. Then watch what happens.

When you bring more "SELF energy" into the relationship, it starts to transform into one that's more calm and connected. Then, *you* can become the change you are hoping to see.

Your Partner's Family of Origin

As you think about your partner's Family of Origin, you may get some insights into why your spouse behaves the way he or she does. You can begin to identify reasons why your spouse may have drinking problems, infidelity issues, difficulty in showing emotions, or a myriad of other choices or patterns that have continued to disappoint you over the years. With awareness and empathy, you will be able to share more peaceful and respectful discussions in the future. A brief review of your and your partner's childhoods can help you foster a sense of compassion for their experience.

Codependence is Not Compassion

"Codependency" is a term that became popularized in the 1980s to describe behavior in alcoholic families where the alcoholic's moods and behaviors affected everyone else. Children learn that their wants and needs aren't as important as "keeping the peace," and adults, they have learned to put others' needs ahead of their own, and eventually they realize your needs matter too. So it is that you may have learned to negate your own needs in order to try to please others.

I often describe codependency to my clients like this: *"I see 'codependence' as a continuum. We are all 'codependent' in some ways. We are all caretakers, givers, nurturers. Where codependence becomes a problem is when taking care of other people's needs is more important than taking care of our own. We often become people pleasers, unable to say "no" or set healthy boundaries. We lose sight of what we want and need as we are constantly trying to meet the needs of others. We make unilateral and unspoken contracts with others as we give and give and give and then get upset when others don't give back to us the same."*

Many of my clients—men and women—have some codependent behaviors that have caused problems in their current relationship. Perhaps you have some too. If so, please be sure to read Melanie Beattie's seminal works *Codependent No More* and *Beyond Codependency*.

When there is dysfunction of any type in a family (addiction, mental illness, family secrets), the children are always affected. For instance, if one or both of your parents were alcoholic, you possibly have some codependent tendencies and came into your marriage as a "Pleaser." After many years of possibly sacrificing your own wants and needs, trying to make your partner happy, you are now wondering, *"What about me? When is it my turn to get my needs met?"*

If your needs weren't met when you were younger, you may have managed your pain with some "Magical Thinking Part" that promised you "someday my prince will come and save me." Then you come to see your prince as a man with foibles and needs of his own, and you become disappointed and angry. Or perhaps you thought you'd marry "the perfect woman" who would make up for the ways your mother may have disappointed you. Then you realize your wife is not going to meet your every need, and you feel unloved.

Whatever you learned in your Family of Origin affected your thoughts about the kind of person you'd like to marry and the kind of person you'd be in that marriage. And then reality set in. As Albert Einstein said, *"Men marry women with the hope they will never change. Women marry men with the hope they will change. Invariably they are both disappointed."*

In my practice, whenever I see someone acting reactively, angrily, or anxiously, I can also see the scared, sad, or hurt Inner Child that's not getting his or her needs met. Often, many of us simply haven't been taught how to ask for what we really want and need, especially in ways that bring us more connection and intimacy. You and your partner may each be managing in ways that aren't truly serving you.

Charlie called and left me an anxious voicemail. He was ready to file for divorce. He liked what he'd read on my website and wanted to do things as a "good guy." But Kathy had threatened to divorce him for eight of their twenty-five years, and he was finally ready to pull the plug. He said, "I'm mad as hell and I don't want to take it anymore!"

"Breathe," I told him. "Just take a breath. You don't have to file today. You don't have to get the attorneys and courts involved right now. Come see me, and I'll teach you a new way to communicate in our first session. And tell your wife you'll be willing to talk about *everything, and we will.*"

If you could look behind your partner's sometimes annoying and hurtful behaviors, you may catch a glimpse of their scared or sad Inner Child. Instead of reacting to your partner with anger, judgment, or blame, take a breath and try to offer compassion. Alice Walker reminds us, *"Be compassionate to everyone. Don't just search for whatever it is that annoys and frightens you—see beyond those things to the basic human being. Especially see **the child in the man or woman**. Even if they are* *destroying you, allow a moment to see how lost in their own delusion and suffering they are."*

Carol and Michael were a couple who went from codependence to compassion, relating from SELF and caring for their own and each other's Inner Child. Carol brought her husband Michael to see me. They had been married for 22 years, with two children. She was very upset when he was in the room, and I wasn't sure what her intention was—counseling or mediation. I spoke with each of them alone for a few minutes, and when it was her turn, she confided in me:

"I feel like I'm lost in the middle of the desert and there are no road signs to be seen."

Carol and Michael had been in a couple's group or couple's therapy for most of their marriage. They wanted to fight less and enjoy each other more, but none of it was working. Carol had thought of leaving but resisted it for years because of their two young children and limited finances. The idea of leaving Michael felt as challenging to her as the idea of staying.

When they first came to see me, Carol believed the only solution was to end the marriage. Michael wished she'd reconsider, but he was reaching the end of his rope, too. His wife had threatened divorce for so long that he finally agreed to discuss it and just end the suffering. Carol felt angry and resentful. She was so unhappy that divorce felt like her only option. She and Michael had stopped having sex years ago. She felt betrayed by his anger and was resistant to any chance of reconciliation.

Carol and Michael were each willing to do their own work to change who they wanted to be in the relationship. Instead of pointing fingers at the other's faults, they looked inside themselves to see how they were being triggered by the other's behaviors.

Carol realized that in her Family of Origin, it was not safe for her to be angry. Her father was an alcoholic, and the family co-dependently revolved around his moods. When he was sober, they were safe. When he was drunk, they needed to stay out of his way. Carol always believed she would find a man who would never get angry and who would be her safe harbor. She learned to manage her own anger by being pleasing and "nice."

When they first met, Michael was very gentle and easy going. Later in their relationship, he would get angry more often, and Carol reacted to it by building a *wall* around her heart to protect herself from another angry man She saw Michael through a *filter* of judgment, and focused on taking care of their children and avoiding being intimate with him.

Michael was at first reluctant to talk about his feelings. He was angry that his wife didn't want to have sex with him, but I could see the hurt underneath. Eventually, he was willing to talk about his Family of Origin. His mother had been the dominant parent, with his father seldom weighing in with any meaningful opinion. Michael wanted to find a partner who would not dictate to him as his mother did to his father. As a child, Michael had to exile his anger, as he didn't want to incur his mother's wrath. As an adult, Michael used his anger as a way to manage his sadness, and he and Carol got more disconnected.

As Carol and Michael listened to each other share deeply and honestly, they were able to have compassion for the other's early life experiences. They became more conscious of their own behaviors and learned how to speak for their exiled parts. Carol shared her anger in a healthy way, and Michael learned to share his sadness. They could both relate with more empathy for the wounds they had caused in each other, and make amends. Carol reflected later,

"In our first session with Linda she shifted the focus away from our tit-for-tat arguments and defensiveness to a focus on each of our selves. Our SELF, she explained, is the essence or core of who each of us is without the hurts of our past, the defensive strategies we've developed to protect ourselves, our fears, worries, etc. All that stuff covers up our shining, beautiful, peaceful, SELF."

After five sessions in, their fighting stopped. Both Carol and Michael were learning to communicate in all the ways they'd hoped they could. Instead of talking about divorce, now they were eagerly focused on improving their sex life and healing those long-held traumas of the past. As Carol explained,

"This happened because we were able to strip away the old resentments and junk, and get a glimpse of the person we each fell in love with all those years ago. After a few short months, we're no longer thinking of ending our marriage. Now we're building an entirely new marriage together. This work was a godsend."

However long you have been with your partner, taking the time to do your own healing work is the best way to transform your relationship—no matter what you decide to do in the future.

Carol and Michael's reconciliation isn't unusual. With Compassionate Communication and Compassionate Mediation, you, too, can revive your marriage—and save it—if you want. And, if your differences can't be resolved, you can learn how to restructure your family with a safe, healthy outcome that meets the needs of everyone with a SELF-Led Divorce.

Questions for You about Your Family of Origin
To help you understand where some of your pain and your partner's pain may have originated, let's focus on your Family of Origin.

Think about your own Family of Origin

- How would you describe your mother?
- How would you describe your father?
- How would you describe their relationship?
- How many siblings do you have?
- What is the birth order?
- How did your birth order affect your life?
- Was there any addiction, abuse, adultery financial strain, illness, divorce, step-family?
- How did everyone get along?
- What are your relationships with your family members today?

What was your *Role* in your Family?

- Were you the first child, second, middle, only, baby?
- Were you the "Family Hero," "Rebel," "Scapegoat," "Forgotten Child?"
- How did you play your Role?
- Did you try to take care of everyone?
- How did you get along with everyone?
- How do you get along with them today?

What were the Rules in your Family?

- Children should be seen and not heard
- Girls should not get angry.
- Boys should not cry.
- Keep family secrets.
- Don't ask for your needs to be met.
- Be perfect.
- Do as you are told.

Now, go through the questions above and answer them about your partner's family.

Next, jot down what you learned from your answers. Examine how your earliest lessons, experiences, and beliefs have shaped who you are now. By the time you've finished, you may begin to have an "aha!" as to why you act a certain way in your relationship. This also can remind each of you to have more compassion for each other's life story. At that point, you may become more caring about your partner's Inner Child, especially once you realize he or she has been carrying his or her burdens for decades.

Every family has some form of challenge that can affect you as a child. Even in families that are considered "perfect" — by themselves and perhaps by others — the pressure to maintain that aura of perfection creates enormous burdens on the children. You are affected by the behaviors you witness. You may have unconsciously adopted certain beliefs and habits from your parents that don't serve you, or reflect your highest SELF. No matter how good a job your parents did for you or you do for your children, there are still "legacy burdens" that are passed down.

It happens to all of us. I was giving a workshop one day, explaining "SELF" and "Parts" to the audience. When I threw out the question, "Where do you think all our limiting beliefs originate?" someone in the back of the room yelled out, "Your parents!" I looked to see who it was. It was my own daughter! So even when we're trying our hardest to do the best we can, we will continue to influence our children just as our parents influenced us. Just knowing this helps us have more compassion for *everyone—including ourselves.*

Walls, Filters, and Other Barriers to Love

You've inherited many of your behaviors, habits, patterns, and beliefs from your Family of Origin, as well as all the experiences you've ever had before meeting your mate. Together, you've co-created the relationship you have now. But you can change it, even if you're the only one reading this. You can *choose* to dismantle the *walls* you "thought" were protecting you from further pain. Because whenever you shut out the possibility of pain, you also shut out the possibility of joy, love, and connection. Once a dam's been built, all those good feelings can't get in (or out). Those walls don't protect you; they actually hurt you. As Deepak Chopra says, *"The less you open your heart to others, the more your heart suffers."*

Then there are the *filters* through which you see your partner. I call them the "always/nevers." You know, "He *always* does that," or "She *never* does this." As my dear friend and mentor, davidji has said, *"As simple as communication seems, much of what we try to communicate to others—and what others try to communicate to us—gets put through all our conditioned filters,* which can cause conflict and frustration in our personal and professional relationships."

If you haven't done the "Find Your Parts" and "Understanding Your Family of Origin" exercises, go back and do them. Like a homing device, they *will* help you uncover your old wounds and judgments, unconscious habits and reactions—all those barriers to love. But you have to be aware of them first, so you can release them and free yourself to love again. Don't beat yourself up or linger in regret. Simply let go of these old patterns with compassion, awareness, and forgiveness—for yourself and your spouse. This is the path that leads you to experience your partner in a whole new way, with a fresh, open heart. The poet Rumi said, *"Your task is not to seek for love, but merely to seek and find all the barriers within yourself that you have built against it."*

Set Healthy Boundaries

As Byron Katie, author of *Loving What Is*, has said, *"The teacher you need is the person you're living with."* Often, it is in your relationships with others that you learn the most about yourself. And, your partner is the best mirror for revealing what's going on inside you. Sometimes your tormentor, (tor-mentor) the person who frustrates you the most, is your greatest teacher; they trigger you so deeply that you're forced to look inside and see where you need to heal or grow.

You and your partner have done the best you knew how— and now you know better, and can do better.

As you're learning to be compassionate with yourself, you will learn how to set healthy boundaries. Sometimes in a relationship you do need to walk away. If there is repeated abuse, addiction, adultery, you may choose to leave rather than endure the pain of staying.

Other times, however, you just need to set clear, firm, and consistent boundaries to reinvent a better relationship for you both. You must learn to say "no" when that's your truth. Get comfortable making room for differences between you and your partner, and navigate them with honesty, empathy, even humor. As you practice this new way of communicating, you will get more of what you want and need.

In his new book, *destressifying*, davidji states that *"Conscious, compassionate communication of your boundaries, feelings and needs creates a greater likelihood that they will be understood, honored and fulfilled."*

When you become more SELF-led, you can heal past wounds and feel safe in the present moment, knowing that you can take better care of yourself now than you could as a child. You no longer need to ruminate on mistakes or perceived insults. You stop projecting into the unknown future all that past pain. You connect to your true self, your highest self, your inner, wisest SELF—and speak with compassion. When you create peace in your own heart, then you can create peace with your partner.

You can do all of this as you learn how to love and appreciate the jobs all your Parts are doing to protect you, and then learn how to unburden the pain of your Inner Child.

Don't Worry about "False Hope"

Laura and Danny were hiding (exiling) their deep pain, vulnerability and fear as they tried to manage their feelings with sarcasm, resentment, and silence. When they were pushed to their limits, they would engage in lingering shouting matches or not speak for days. They continued to see each other through their *filters* of judgment, blame, and disdain. They built *walls* around their heart to protect themselves from being hurt over and over again by the other's words or indifference. Now and then, they'd each try to peer over their walls to see if the other was changing. Not only were they each afraid of being hurt again, they were also afraid to give one another "the wrong idea."

Laura and Danny were hiding (exiling) their deep pain, vulnerability and fear as they tried to manage their feelings with sarcasm, resentment and silence. When they were pushed to their limits, they would engage in lingering shouting matches or not speak for days. They continued to see each other through their *filters* of judgment, blame, and disdain. They built *walls* around their heart to protect themselves from being hurt over and over again by the other's words or indifference. Now and then, they'd each try to peer over their walls to see if the other was changing. Not only were they each afraid of being hurt again, they were also afraid to give one another "the wrong idea."

Many of my clients know that they are holding onto their anger as a way of arming themselves against staying in their painful relationship. They are afraid that if they put down their walls and "act nice" to their partner, then there will be a sense of "false hope"—from the partner (or their children)—

and that no decision will be made to leave. They are concerned that it will look like they are content, when they are not, and are willing to stick it out, when they want to leave. They see their "wall" as a protector, and they don't trust themselves enough to put the wall down and be a source of love and compassion in their family. When you learn to live "in SELF," you don't need the walls. Instead you have appropriate boundaries that allow you to interact in healthy ways.

A *boundary* clearly identifies what you will and will not allow into your personal space. A *wall* around your heart is often a defensive reaction to pain. Your *filters* carry your judgments, which may cloud your clear present moment awareness. As davidji says, "*Healthy boundaries protect us and allow nourishing experience to enter and expand us. Walls try to protect us and don't let the good in or even the bad out.*

Laura had been angry for years because Danny had disappointed her with his unilateral financial decisions that put them in precarious circumstances. Danny was working hard to reverse the problems, but Laura didn't want to let him off the hook as she believed he would not work as hard to correct his mistakes.

She felt she was done with the relationship and she would divorce him as soon as the financial situation improved. She didn't want to give him (or their children) "false hope" that things between them could improve. So she stayed angry, walled, and resentful.

If you are close to ending your relationship and moving on, you might not want to try again. You may have considered life alone and even idealized what it would be like. Or you've given up on counseling because *now* it's so bad that no one would blame you for leaving. But what if you both tried harder and it still wasn't enough? How could you leave if your partner made some improvements, but it still wasn't enough to make you happy?

Here's the truth: You can always get a divorce. Even if you're kinder and more compassionate, even if you have sex again, you can still end the relationship. The other party (and your children and everyone who loves you) will probably always hope you get back together, even years later.

Learning how to communicate from your highest SELF is the first and fastest way to resolve your issues.

The "worst-case scenario" (or "best case") is that you fall back in love and create a new life together. Or you learn a new way to communicate that allows you to become the best co-parents you can be. What do you have to lose by trying again? At least, you can always look back and know you did the *best* you could.

> Laura finally realized that she was hurting herself as much as she was hurting her husband, and her children. She realized it was difficult for her to stay so reactive, as she knew herself to be an essentially loving and generous person. She learned how to speak more from her higher SELF, and talk about her sadness, fear and disappointment rather than have to armor herself with judgment, blame and resentment.

When you have your individual needs and desires understood, then you're more willing to put down your swords and shields, and open the door to invite more peace and compassion into your relationship.

David Simon, author and co-founder of the Chopra Center, wrote in his book, *Free to Love, Free to Heal*, "*Boundary setting can be learned, but it requires awareness and practice. One established, healthy boundaries protect us from harm while allowing nourishing experience to enter an expand us. If your caregivers, like so many, were deficient in these core skills, you will most likely need some emotional healing work....helping us re-parent our inner child.*

It is my experience that healing our inner parents *is just as important, if we are to release the old emotional residue that is binding our heart, and become free to love and free to heal."*

As you do your healing work, you'll be able to get in touch with what's important to you moving forward. You'll be able to remember what it is you truly want and need when you practice the Five Steps that follow.

Chapter 3
Five Steps to Get What You Want and Need

"Every day brings new choices."
—Martha Beck, Author

Most people who come to see me start their session by telling me all the problems in the relationship and everything that they don't want to put up with anymore. Perhaps you've been focusing for a very long time on what you don't want or all the things you will never tolerate again. You may have lost sight of what you truly want—both in the present and for the future.

The Five Steps that follow will help you focus on what you would like to create—alone or together. As Eleanor Roosevelt said, *"In the long run, we shape our lives, and we shape ourselves. The process never ends until we die. And the choices we make are ultimately our own responsibility."* You can begin to make your new choices from your highest and best SELF.

When you learn how to put these Five Steps into practice, you will find that your communication improves exponentially. You will focus on what is truly important to you and set positive intentions, which will help you attract and manifest more of what you desire.

5 Steps to Get What You Want and Need

(1) **Remember** what you want and need

(2) Know that you **deserve** what you want and need

(3) Learn how to **ask** for it

(4) Be willing to **receive**

(5) Stay **grateful**

(1) The first step is to *realize and remember* what you truly want and need.
It may be difficult for you to describe what you want and need right now. When you first began your relationship, you might have been focused on "pleasing" and doing things that would make your partner happy. Perhaps you were young or still reacting from an earlier relationship. Whatever your history, you entered this current relationship hoping that you could both meet each other's needs. Somewhere along the line you lost sight of what you really wanted. You may have lost sight of your own needs because you were so busy taking care of everyone else's.

Perhaps you may have become too focused on all those things that you *don't* want that you haven't really been clear lately on what you *do* want. You may have given up hope because you have felt ignored or dismissed, and you are now reluctant to ask anymore.

Be willing to take this first step. Make a list of what you want in your relationship, in your family, in your life. By setting your intentions, you set the course for a whole new experience. You can make your list in any way, at any time. Go for a walk. Allow your mind to wander to things that made you happy as a child.

Just write a list, stream of consciousness. You can make a "vision board" or "treasure map." Cut pictures and words out of magazines that capture the energy or essence you'd like to feel in your life. When you meditate, ask the Universe to provide signs of who you are, what you want and what's your purpose. What would bring you joy and happiness? Learning what you want and need is the first step. And focusing on the feelings—more love, peace, joy, happiness, connection—will help you plan what you want to do next.

As Danielle LaPorte says in her book, *The Desire Map,* "*What if your core desired feelings consciously informed how you plan your day, your year—your life? You know what will happen with that kind of inner clarity and outer action? You'll feel the way you want to feel more often than not. Decisions will be easier to make. You'll know what to say 'No, thank you" to and what to say "Hell, yes!" to. I bet you'll complain less. You'll be more optimistic, more openhearted. It will be easier for you to return to your center in the midst of a challenge."*

As you become clear on how you'd like to *feel*, it will also help you make choices and take inspired action in the direction of manifesting your deepest desires in all areas of your life. At the Chopra Center, you are invited to ask yourself these soul questions before you meditate. You can begin to pose the questions now.

The Soul Questions

(1) Who am I?

(2) What do I truly want?

(3) What is my *dharma* or purpose? (i.e., How can I use my unique gifts and talents to help and to serve?)

(4) For what am I grateful?

Take a deep breath, and *let go of the questions*—and let the Universe work out the details. If you stay *present* and *aware*, you may synchronistically find miracles everywhere!

(2) The second step is to know that you *deserve* what you want and need.

This is often the most challenging step to do on your own. You may have some baggage from your Family of Origin and other experiences in your past that keep you from knowing how deserving you are of happiness. You may have been criticized as a child. You may have had some traumatic experiences that made you feel worthless, victimized, or not good enough. Your self-esteem may be suffering.

You can unburden all those traumas and limiting beliefs, but it may take some outside support. I want to remind you that you are Divine. In this moment, as you are, no matter what you are doing, have done, or plan to do, you are a perfect incarnation of the Divine. You are complete. There is nothing more you need to do. In fact, doing less would probably help. There is nothing bad, wrong, or inadequate about you. You are *not broken*. You may be *burdened*. You can *unburden*, heal your wounds, and remember the light that shines so brightly underneath your pain.

There are ways to unburden pain from the past and not bring it into your future.

(3) The third step is to learn how to *ask* for what you want and need.

As you *know* what you want and need and finally realize you *deserve* it, then you become willing to *ask* for it in a whole new way. You won't have to hide your truth or walk on eggshells. You won't have to demand or yell or nag or whine. You won't have to threaten or demean. You can calmly and respectfully ask your spouse for what it is you want and need without rancor, anger, sarcasm, judgment or blame.

Just notice. When you're asking for something, and you know that you deserve it and can calmly ask what you want, your tone and your voice will come from a much more loving place. Learning the skills of Compassionate Communication and the Miracle of Empathy (see Chapter 4) shifts the dynamics from the habitual reactions you both have had to possibility and hopefulness.

You may not get all that you request, but you will receive more than if you never ask. Also, when you speak from SELF, rather than from angry or resentful or entitled Parts, your partner listens in a whole new way. When you are coming from SELF and speaking *for* your Parts rather than *from* your Parts, you offer a safe environment for a dialogue. Remember, to make your point, it's not *what* you say, but *how* you say it.

(4) The fourth step is to be willing to *receive*.

Once you remember what you want and need, truly know that you deserve it, ask for it with honesty, empathy and respect, the next step is to learn how to *receive*. This is often difficult for many people, because they have learned or come to believe that their identity and external validation comes only when giving to others.

You may believe somewhere deep inside that self-care is selfish and you become too vulnerable or indebted when you're receiving something. Again, those are old beliefs from burdened Parts that have a limited perspective based on your past.

As you give yourself the love, acceptance, appreciation, and validation that you have always wanted, you will find it easier to receive from others. You begin to recognize that giving and receiving are all a part of the flow of the Universe and you must allow others the gift of giving to you just as you enjoy the gift of giving to them.

(5) The fifth step is to stay *grateful* for everything that you do receive.

Even if your partner can't meet all your needs—*and no one can*—you can be grateful for what they have given you. You can be grateful if he or she is willing to listen to you with empathy and be open to change.

Gratitude is staying in the present moment with awareness of all the miracles and blessings you already have. The more you stay in gratitude—the more you are "in SELF"— the more your partner will be attracted to the beautiful essence of who you truly are. He or she can put down the defensive walls that have built up, and then choose to connect with you in more intimate and meaningful ways. You will begin to experience a new relationship filled with more grace.

As you learn these Five Steps and share your desires with your partner, the following chapter on the Miracle of Empathy will help you negotiate a whole new partnership. When you communicate from your true or highest SELF, you stop using extreme behaviors to distract or numb you. You no longer have to manage your feelings without being able to express yourself. You learn to have the courage and confidence to ask for what you need, set appropriate boundaries and feel safe no matter what the outcome of your request.

Chapter 4
Experience the Miracle of Empathy

*"What you want to create is a bridge of empathy through which
both of you understand what's in each other's hearts
rather than what's in your heads."*
— davidji, Author

What if you could talk about all the issues that divide you with empathy and connection? How would you like to find a safe way to heal your conflicts about money, parenting, work, play, vacation, families, friendships, and even sex? Wouldn't that be terrific? That's the future that could be possible for you. You can resolve all your differences and feel partnered, supported, understood and validated. As Meryl Streep has said, *"The great gift of human beings is that we have the power of empathy."*

The "Miracle of Empathy" practice will give you and your partner a chance to feel heard, understood and empathized with on a much deeper level than ever before. It will also give you the opportunity to co-create a new relationship based on who you are now, as well as what you want and need from this moment forward. You can begin a new relationship as you negotiate changes you would like to see in the future.

Empathy isn't always easy to offer and doesn't always happen. If you're like many people in a contentious relationship, instead of being compassionate you've learned how to push each other's buttons. You've triggered repeated and defensive reactions.

What needs to happen is your walls around your heart need to come down safely, your buttons need to be removed gently, and the triggers need to be released and put aside. It's time to partner in a whole new way because you're on the same team!

When you've been hurt in the past, you began to see your partner through the filter of the judgments you made about how their behavior affected you. The pain often mirrors the ways in which you were hurt as a child. Each painful experience with your partner adds bricks to the wall you build to defend yourself from being vulnerable again.

Just like a filter on a heater needs to be changed so that clean air can flow, every so often you need to change the filter through which you see your partner. Just put in a new one, a fresh one, a present-day one, that isn't muddied by the past.

You can TAKE A BREATH—even *one* conscious breath—come back to the present moment, in your body, not your mind, and see that the person in front of you is possibly trying to love you the best way they know how.

Professor of philosophy Sam Keen said, *"It's not about finding a 'perfect person' to love. It's learning how to perfectly love another imperfect person."*

Speaking *for* Your Exiles *from* Your SELF

You and your partner are both beautiful Souls having a human experience. Each of you is affected by your past. When you have empathy for the other's experience and perspective, you can each make changes in how you relate and respond. When you are "in SELF," you learn how to listen with empathy as you speak honestly about all of your feelings. You find the courage to speak your truth, calmly, and listen with compassion to the feelings of your partner.

When you practice the Miracle of Empathy, you learn to use "I" messages. You talk about your own exiled feelings. You talk about your hurt, your sadness, your fears, even your anger, but you do it in a way that doesn't blame or judge your partner. (When you are speaking *for* your Part, there is a different energy than when you are *blended* with a Part.)

You learn how to listen so that you truly understand the perspective of your spouse. *(For the sake of easier reading, I will interchange the feminine and masculine pronouns.)* You may not always *agree* with what she says, but you let her know that you truly *understand* what she's feeling. Then you let her know that you get it. You heard it, you understood it, and you take her feelings and needs into your heart. If you've done something to hurt her you're sorry, and if you're listening from a place of compassion, you offer that so that she feels truly heard and understood.

One honest "I'm sorry" for actions (or inactions) that caused pain can save thousands of dollars in attorney fees, minimize damage to children, and create an atmosphere that fosters resolution. One heartfelt "thank you" allows miracles to occur.

Marshall Rosenberg explained the interactive nature of empathy in his seminal book *Nonviolent Communication*. *"We need empathy to give empathy…if we want them to hear us we would need first to empathize with them. The more we empathize with what leads them to behave in the ways they are not meeting our needs, the more likely it is that they will be able to reciprocate afterwards."*

When you begin to reflect and receive more understanding, you are then more willing to create reasonable compromises that meet both of your needs. As you find the courage to safely share your feelings, you will use these Compassionate Communication techniques to co-create a new marriage together, or to become respectful co-parents or friends if you decide to separate or divorce.

Using "I" Messages Avoids Guilt, Blame, and Judgment

Learning how to speak *for* your Parts, instead of *from* your Parts, will allow you to talk about your sadness, hurt, and fear. As your partner listens, understands and empathizes, the Parts of both of you calm down and healing begins.

Listening from SELF—Hear, Understand, and Empathize

When you pay attention to your partner's feelings, he feels seen and validated. When someone feels understood, his Parts can calm down and healing can begin.

The Miracle of Empathy
An Exercise in Communication
*(With gratitude to
Harville Hendrix and Richard Schwartz)*

PARTNER A REQUESTS A CONVERSATION
PARTNER A says to PARTNER B:
"I have something to discuss with you. Is now a good time?

PARTNER B RESPONDS:
"Yes," (or picks an alternate time that same day).

PARTNER A shares feelings and speaks from SELF and says:
"When (something happens/ed), I feel/felt (exile), (exile), and (exile).

The use of the Exiles invites empathy. The use of Managers and Extreme Parts challenges your partner's Parts to engage.

PARTNER B LISTENS and HEARS and says:
I HEAR you say that "when (something happens/ed), you feel/ felt (exile), and (exile)."

Use the same words. Repeat the message verbatim.

"Is that right?"

PARTNER A either acknowledges it is right, or repeats the message.

PARTNER B UNDERSTANDS and says:

I UNDERSTAND that "when (something happens/ed), you feel/felt (exile), (exile), and (exile)."
PARTNER B pauses a moment to let the understanding response be acknowledged.

PARTNER B SHOWS EMPATHY and says:

"I am sorry."(*An apology for something she has done or not done, or just a true empathetic understanding of A's feelings.*)

I don't want you to feel that way.

I want to learn a new way for us to communicate.

I am sorry."

(Embellish in any way that feels sincere. Let your partner know that you hear how s/he feels, you understand, and you care.)

PARTNER A is GRATEFUL and says:

"Thank you.

In the future, I would prefer W, X or, Y (behavior changes)."

PARTNER B ACKNOWLEDGES:

"I can do one or more of those, or perhaps we can try Z."

PARTNERS A and B:
COMMUNICATE, NEGOTIATE. CONNECT.

As Speaker (A):
Notice the timing of your requests for attention.

If you are trying to initiate a conversation with your partner, make sure you begin the dialogue by asking, *"Is now a good time?"* You want to make sure your partner is as much "in SELF" as possible. If he is busy or preoccupied or overwhelmed with something else, he will not be able to give you the attention or empathy you want.

Use "I" Messages.

When you want to express your feelings, know that you deserve to have the feelings, without a need to explain why. Often you may try to point out what you think your partner is doing that is "wrong" (which comes across as blaming and judgmental) in order to avoid talking about your feelings (and being honest, open and vulnerable).

You might have said, "If you didn't do this, I wouldn't feel this way, so YOU need to change!" You would rather try to change your partner to meet your needs than learn to be honest about how you feel and what you want and need. However, when you judge your partner and all that is heard is criticism, she will listen from a place of defensiveness and rebuttal, rather than being open from her higher SELF.

Speak FOR Your Exiles.

You learn to speak FOR your sadness, hurt, fear, anger. You don't need to blame your partner for causing you to feel that way. Just calmly and clearly share what are your true feelings. You will learn how to use "I" messages as you talk about your own feelings, not focusing on the "you messages" that talk about the other person's behavior. Instead of saying, "You are always mean to me." You say, "When you raise your voice, *I feel* sad and hurt."

State your feelings in as succinct a way as possible. You don't need to go into detail as to "why" you feel the way you feel. Just express it. The more detail you offer, the less able your partner will be to stay in SELF. Your "story" about why you feel the way you do will trigger his or her need to fact-check, set the record straight, defend himself or herself.

So just say, *"When something happens (or happened),"* *I feel (or felt) sad, scared, or hurt."* If you never get angry, it is healthy to begin to talk about it when your boundaries have been violated. Usually, couples have been mired in anger for a long time and have learned to ignore each other's anger. You will often get more empathy when you are strong enough to be vulnerable, and talk about your hurt, sadness, fears.

Appreciate Whatever Empathy is Attempted.

The speaker (A) says "thank you" for the empathy shown. Don't judge the level of empathy or whether it's enough to make up for the past, just be grateful your partner is willing to learn a new way to communicate. First say *"thank you,"* and after your gratitude, you can then ask for a change in behavior in the future. Remember there will be a learning curve, and the more receptive you are to your partner's attempt at empathy, the more empathy you will eventually receive

Ask for What You Want and Need.

Using the skills you've learned in the "Five Steps to Get What You Want and Need," you'll now know what you *do* want instead of what you *don't* want.

Negotiate a behavior change that would be helpful.

Think of behaviors that you would welcome in the future. When you are in SELF you can calmly and confidently ask for what you desire—as you remember you *deserve* to have your needs met, and so does your partner. This is when you'll begin to negotiate the behaviors you would like to share in your relationship in the future. You may not get everything you want, but at least begin a dialogue that makes room for your partner's feeling and needs as well.

As Listener (B):

Listen from Your SELF.

When you are listening from SELF, you are *compassionate* about your partner's experience and *curious* to learn more. You do not try to explain, rationalize, or defend your actions. You may be thinking, *"If only my partner understood why I said what I said or did what I did, she wouldn't have to feel so sad, scared, angry."* Or, you don't want to feel guilty about what you did or didn't do, and try to justify your choices. No matter what Parts of you get triggered by your partner's sharing, just listen patiently from your highest SELF.

All your partner needs is for you to listen, understand, and empathize. Once he feels that you truly *get it*, he can finally *let it go*. You'll feel the same when your partner learns how to give empathy to you. You might feel that it's been too long in coming and it's not enough empathy, but start wherever you can and build on that.

Open Your Heart as Much as Possible.

Remember that your partner is truly in pain, and no matter what she has said to you or about you in the past, she is trying to show up and be honest, open and vulnerable, and is hoping and trusting you to be kind and compassionate.

Ask Your "Yes, but's" to Separate.

As you listen to your partner, you will want to lessen his pain by wanting him to understand that you didn't mean to hurt him. You'll want to offer, a "yes, but" as he is speaking. This is the time to ask those Parts to let you listen from SELF. Let those Parts know that they can be expressed at a later time.

The Parts of you that want to explain, justify, deny, qualify, or in any way mitigate the pain will instead be stealing focus from your partner's feelings and taking it back for yourself. So ask your Parts to "step back" and let you show up in SELF. When it's your turn to talk about your feelings, you can then add the message these Parts want to convey.

Pay Close Attention to What You Hear.

Try not to listen from a Part that wants to check the facts or debate the issues. Pay attention to what your partner is saying. Repeat the words verbatim. Check with your partner to make sure you've got the right words.

You can "actively listen" by repeating what has been shared to reflect that you are listening closely. As you become more advanced in this process, you can ask your partner to "tell me more," and invite him to share even more authenticity and honesty with you. He can then go more deeply into his feelings and communicate more intimately.

Try to understand the other's point of view, even if you don't agree. Convey that understanding as compassionately as possible.

Put Up Your "Psychic Umbrella."

I often suggest that you try to put up your "psychic umbrella" and just observe the Parts of your partner, without needing to take them in or be triggered by them. The "umbrella" is just an imaginary protection that protects you from "taking in" the energy of your partner's Parts. You just witness calmly without the need to react.

Ask Your Parts to Separate.

As you listen to your partner express her feelings and needs, you may notice that you feel defensive, critical of yourself or your partner, afraid of what she will say next, sad about hurting her, guilty, judgmental. You may want to respond to help your partner feel better. You can gently ask your Parts to "relax" or "step back" and let you, in SELF, show up to hear what your partner has to say. It is the beginning of a new relationship based on calm, compassionate empathy.

Listen, Understand, Offer Empathy.

You *listen* to the words your partner is using (as he learns to use "I" messages about his feelings—not his judgments of you.) You can repeat back the words to make sure that he knows you are truly paying attention to what he is sharing with you. You next reflect your *understanding* of what he says, whether you agree or not.

Again, you are showing him acceptance of his experience without his needing to justify why he feel the way he does. This understanding is very important. If you just say "I'm sorry" without indicating that you truly know what you are sorry for, he will feel that you are placating him. Or you've said the words many times and then continued with the same behavior that caused the pain in the first place. When you truly understand how hurt your partner is, you can fully commit to making changes so that he doesn't feel that way anymore.

Make Amends or Offer Compassion

If there is something you did (or didn't do) that hurt your partner, then a heartfelt apology is always appreciated. Saying "I'm sorry," when you truly are will do wonders for your relationship. And repeat as often as necessary.

If you haven't done something specific to cause your partner's feelings, you can still compassionately be "sorry" for the other's feeling as you convey your care and empathy.

Be Willing to Hear a Request for a Behavior Change.

Agree where you can, or negotiate something else. You can creatively co-create a new way of relating that meets both your needs.

A Summary of the Miracle of Empathy

As the speaker who is requesting empathy:

Use "I" messages instead of talking about (or to) another.

Notice the timing of your requests for attention.

State your feelings in as succinct a way as possible.

Appreciate whatever empathy is attempted.

Ask for a behavior change that would be helpful.

Be willing to negotiate a compromise.

As the listener who is offering empathy:

Open your heart as much as possible.

Ask your "yes, but's" to separate while you listen. *(Let them know they'll have a chance to be heard.)*

Pay close attention to what you hear.

Repeat your partner's words verbatim.

Check to make sure you've got the right words.

Try to understand the other's point of view, even if you don't agree.

Convey that understanding as much as possible.

Make amends ("I'm sorry") when there is something you have or haven't done for which you can apologize.

Compassionately be "sorry" for the other's feelings

Be willing to hear a request for a behavior change.

Agree where you can, or negotiate something else.

A new relationship with your partner is possible once you learn how to communicate from your highest and best SELF. As you learn and practice the Miracle of Empathy, you will be able to use it in all the conversations in Compassionate Mediation. Feelings from the past can be acknowledged and healed, as you have more tools to create decisions for your future.

.

When Compassion for Your Partner is a Challenge

The key to creating a new relationship is compassion— compassion for yourself, and compassion for your partner. You begin to realize that you've both done the best you knew how to do according to your history and your level of awareness at the time. You learn how to set healthy boundaries, take the time to understand and unburden your Parts, and access more inner peace.

However, some relationships are more difficult to navigate owing to heightened challenges presented by such issues as abuse, addiction, attention deficit disorder (ADD or ADHD), extra-relationship affairs, Asperger's syndrome, mental illness, high sensitivity (HSP), and more.

Abuse or Mental Illness

If you don't have peace because there's truly emotional or physical abuse, you may have to leave, even temporarily, until safety can be maintained. Make sure you are safe and plan to engage in Compassionate Mediation only if you trust that your spouse won't be hurtful. If you believe that there is some mental illness, it must be addressed, as medication can possibly save your relationship.

Medication can help alleviate the symptoms of mania (which can come out as anger or rage) and depression. However, many people with bipolar disorder are either undiagnosed on non-adherent when it comes to taking their prescribed medications. Their outbursts or mood swings have created havoc in the marriage, and the spouse is often left feeing angry, hurt and stuck. Compassionate Mediation can offer other options.

Sometimes the possibility of divorce is the only motivating factor that would inspire adherence with taking the medication. Usually, there have been years of arguing and threatening, withdrawing, or avoiding. When you meet the issue head on—"Please take your medication or I will have to leave"—and you follow through on a discussion of what leaving would look and feel like, changes do happen.

Maria was determined to divorce Ryan because she could no longer live with his angry outbursts and mood swings. She had tried for years to make excuses, turn the other cheek, forgive and forget. She finally couldn't take it anymore. She knew that he was probably bipolar, but he wouldn't agree and refused to do anything about it.

When Maria told Ryan that she wanted to look at the possibility of divorce, he finally realized she was no longer just going to complain and forgive. Unless he learned how to deal with the problem, he was going to lose his family. He finally went to see a psychiatrist and began to take the medication regularly.

Addiction

If there is an addiction, then please go to a 12-Step Program (Alcoholics Anonymous, Narcotics Anonymous, Al-Anon) and get help for coping, communicating, and being present in a way that can stay loving without judgment. You will learn how to connect to your Higher Power as you "let go and let God." You will be able to "take your own inventory" and pay attention to what you are saying and doing instead of what your partner is doing and say. You may realize when you are being controlling, judgmental, hyper-vigilant.

Greg was furious that his wife wouldn't acknowledge how her drinking was destroying their relationship and affecting their children. Whenever he came to see me, he could barely contain his rage. He wanted to vent in my office and hope that I could get through to her so that she would see the light and change.

No matter how often I recommended that Greg go to Al-Anon, he refused. He kept justifying his reasons for being mad, and she kept seeing his outbursts as controlling and abusive. Their possibly respectful separation devolved into a series of threats, which eventually sent them to their attorneys who could continue the fight.

The success of Compassionate Mediation is directly related to your ability to do your own work on getting to SELF. If you are going to maintain a demeanor of complaint, judgment, and blame, you will get more of those directed at you. If you are willing to look at the changes you can make first, you have a much better chance of success.

On the other hand, another couple was able to weather the healing that happens when addiction is addressed and each spouse gets their own support. When each member of the relationship is willing to focus on how they can change themselves, instead of changing the other, transformation happens.

Brian had been using drugs and alcohol for five years before he and his wife Donna came to see me. She was shut down and angry; he was still hiding his drug use and pretending to be available for counseling.

Eventually, he got into a 30-day program and came home to restart his life. By that time, Donna had put up so many walls around her heart that she felt hopeless she could ever care for him the same way again. She had felt so hurt, wounded, ignored, and unloved for so long that anger, sarcasm, and resentment were her modes of defense.

However, Donna was loving enough and wise enough to know that she needed to do her own healing, just as Brian was doing his. She got herself to her first Al-Anon meeting, and her life changed.

She learned how to work the same 12 steps that her husband was working in his meetings. She was powerless over changing him. She learned how to trust a Higher Power (which can be members of the meeting), and she took her own "inventory." She learned how to recognize when she was being sarcastic, angry, judgmental, hyper-vigilant, and then to share that self-awareness. She was able to make amends and keep doing the best she could do to become more compassionate and caring.

She brought her highest SELF back into the relationship, allowed herself to talk about her sadness, anger, fear, and pain, and the two of them began a brand new relationship together with the compassionate wisdom of each of their highest and best SELF.

Adult ADD (Attention Deficit Disorder) or ADHD (Attention Deficit Hyper-Activity Disorder)

Aside from abuse or addiction, some issues may be more subtle. Many couples come to me with complaints that mirror the symptoms of Adult ADD or ADHD. One member is often scattered and non-reliable, while the other party feels exhausted from being responsible for all the details of their lives.

If this sounds familiar, you may want to learn more about adult ADD/ADHD and how it may be affecting your relationship. Living with someone with ADD/ADHD can be challenging for both of you, but learning about it can be healing.

Connie came to see me determined to divorce her husband Sam, whom I recognized as someone with Adult ADD. Connie complained that Sam was terrible with finances, always late to places, and couldn't keep from cluttering the house. Connie had given bills to Sam to mail and then found them in his pants pocket long after the due dates.

Connie took it as a personal affront that whenever Sam left for work every day, he would forget to close the garage door behind him. Each time she had to close it, she told herself, *"He doesn't love me. He doesn't care about what I tell him. He doesn't listen to me. My needs aren't getting met. I have to leave."*

I know there were other problems in the marriage that weren't only about the garage door, but it indicated to me that Connie knew nothing about the ADD that affected Sam his entire life. It's a challenge to have ADD and it's a different kind of burden to be married to someone with ADD.

If you are the spouse, you feel that all the responsibilities are on your shoulders, and your partner drops the ball when you want to count on him (or her). If you take the time to learn about Adult ADD/ADHD, and to discuss the effects of it with compassion and empathy, you and your partner can make accommodations based on your mutual awareness and consideration. Research ADD and ADHD and share what you learn with your partner. Then you can reframe your problems and find solutions. Instead of being resentful for what you don't have, you stay grateful for what you do have together.

Unfortunately, Connie and Sam didn't want to do that work, so they finished their divorce. In other cases, a spouse can lovingly close the garage door and be grateful he has a partner willing to help support the family by going to work. Or as the other spouse, you can put a Post-it® note reminder to "shut the garage door" on the car dashboard and remind yourself to help your spouse feel loved each day!

Educating yourself about the effects of ADD and ADHD on your relationship is the first step to healing. As John Gray says in his book, *Staying Focused in a Hyper World*, *"Without focus, communication breaks down in all relationships and frustration increases. In romantic relationships, passion is lost while breakups and divorce continue to rise."*

If your partner is willing to learn about the effects of ADD/ADHD on your relationship and to take steps to rectify the problems with medication or behavior modifications, then a new relationship together will be possible. Sometimes the awareness that you are unhappy enough to consider leaving the marriage is the catalyst for real change to occur. When you share your feelings from your highest SELF, your calm, compassionate presence creates a safe space for healing and change. Your partner can hear you in a whole new way.

HSP

An HSP is a Highly Sensitive Person. Elaine Aron has pioneered the understanding of the patterns of HSP and how it affects individuals and couples. According to Aron, as well as other researchers, *"Highly sensitive people, who compose about a fifth of the population (equal numbers in men and women), may process sensory data much more deeply and thoroughly due to a biological difference in their nervous systems. This is a specific trait…that in the past has often been confused with innate shyness, social anxiety problems, social inhibition, social phobia and innate fearfulness, and introversion."*

More awareness of these HSP traits and tendencies allows for compassion and accommodation rather than judgment and reactivity. If an HSP is married to somebody who is not an HSP or to someone who likes a lot of activity, the spouses have to find a way to accommodate each other and communicate with compassion.

Diane came to see me alone, planning to divorce her husband, Larry. She didn't think she could ever make him happy. He always complained that she "was too much of a hermit," "spent too much time alone," and didn't have the energy to keep up with the social life he wanted them to share.

Diane had never heard of HSP, and when she realized that it described her, she began to cry. She wasn't crying because she was disappointed. She cried because she was relieved. As she told me, *"For the first time in my life, I don't feel crazy. I have always felt there was something wrong with me, and I felt guilty that I didn't want to do as much as my husband. I needed time alone, in my bed, and I believed him when he told me I was depressed and needed medication. I don't feel I'm depressed, but I realize now, if I give myself the time I need to relax and rejuvenate, without feeling bad about it, I'll have more energy to spend with Larry in ways we both enjoy."*

She went home and shared Elaine Aron's books and research and was able to negotiate a new relationship with her husband. She tried to be more social when she could, and he had more patience and understanding when she needed "down time."

He would then make plans for himself and would come back home happy and loving.

In learning about HSP, Diane was able to accept Parts of herself that she had judged, hidden and regretted shamefully. She and her husband offered each other more empathy and compassion based on their new awareness.

Understanding yourself and your partner is one of the first steps to negotiating a new and more loving relationship.

Navigating After an Affair

If you or your spouse has had an emotional of physical affair, there is much pain to heal. Sex and affairs can be potent Extreme behaviors to which people resort when their Parts are overloaded. An affair can seem to take your mind off all of your problems. The endorphins that are released when you think you are "in love" anesthetizes you to the pain and sadness and anger you feel in relation to your partner. You "exit" the relationship even though you are physically present. Even if you don't feel "in love," the excitement or newness of the affair may seem to mitigate the pain of the marriage.

In order to see if there is any future in your troubled relationship at home, you must end the affair and focus on only one relationship at a time. If you try to do both, you cannot fully explore either.

You can't lose what you are meant to have. If your "new love" can't give you the space or time to work through your issues at home, then you will know that you are not loved unconditionally, and you may always have to jump through hoops. If you are afraid your new love will find someone else in the meantime, then you haven't lost anything of value, and it's better to learn that sooner than later.

The three things that the partner who had the affair needs to do are:

1) End the relationship immediately and avoid all future contact.
2) Be sincerely remorseful for the pain caused.
3) Be willing to be patient for as long as necessary until the other party has time to rebuild trust.

The partner who has felt betrayed needs to:

1) Recognize his/her contribution to the situation *before* the affair.
2) Do her/his own work towards forgiveness.
3) Be willing to take the time to trust again and be as kind as possible.

The Miracle of Empathy practice in Compassionate Mediation gives you tools to discuss all the issues that preceded the affair, as well as make joint plans for the future based on compassion and mutual respect.

Know Thyself

The more you know yourself, the better you are able to relate to your partner. It's in a relationship that you can learn the most about yourself. So thank each other for showing up to help you learn what you are meant to know. If you don't take the time to heal your issues now, you will leave your current relationship and go find someone similar until you master the lessons that will help you grow.

Your partner is a mirror of what's going on inside of you. As you change internally, you will invite a different reflection of yourself into your life. Either your partner will change and grow to better reflect you, or you may need to part ways and each find a relationship that is better suited to who you are now.

However, if separation is the ultimate decision you both make, you can do it from SELF, instead of a reactive Part. When you come from SELF, your communication can be honest, calm and even loving. You can then plan together how to restructure your relationship or how to end it and move on. You can co-create a fulfilling relationship that endures throughout the hardships, boredom, and challenges that you face as you age. The answer is in communication.

How can you learn to express yourself compassionately and listen with empathy so that you and your partner feel met and understood? davidji reminds us, *"Many issues we're struggling with right now regarding another person—such as holding a grudge, being passive aggressive, not feeling treated well, delaying a difficult conversation, having schadenfreude, being in a fight, giving them the silent treatment, and so on—can be destressified by having a conscious conversation."*

As you become more SELF-led, you'll be better able to have a conscious conversation about your future. Sometimes you have to be fully informed of the alternatives before you can commit to truly creating something deeper and more meaningful with your partner today. That is where Compassionate Mediation can help.

SECTION TWO
Compassionate Mediation
Become Your Own Best Advocate

Chapter 5
Explore All Your Options

*"Whatever the present moment contains,
accept it as if you had chosen it.
Always work with it, not against it.
Make it your friend and ally, not your enemy.
This will miraculously transform your whole life."*
.'—Eckhart Tolle, Author

You can explore the possibility of creating a new marriage with your spouse before you decide to divorce. As you progress through the process of Compassionate Mediation, you'll learn how to communicate from your highest, best SELF. You'll begin to understand and accept all Parts of yourself (your anger, sadness, fear, ambivalence, resistance, etc.) and your partner's. You'll acquire the necessary clarity, confidence, and courage to speak for your Parts and to listen with empathy as your partner does the same. You'll be able to respectfully talk about all the rights and responsibilities that you each must assume as you move forward—with compassion.

Individuals and couples who've learned how to do this often heal past wounds, forgive each other, and create a new relationship based on who they are *now* and what they both need moving forward. Compassionate Mediation can help you—no matter where you are in your relationship right now.

Before choosing divorce, you should consider all other possible choices. Ask your partner to go with you for marital counseling or seek therapy for yourself. You might separate for a while without any legal action, or finally decide to end your marriage.

Consider Counseling as a Possibility

There are many different forms of counseling, with many different techniques and goals. Individual counseling helps you get clear on your own thoughts and behaviors. Couples counseling (or marital counseling) offers a forum for you and your spouse to weigh in on all the issues between you. Group therapy allows you to benefit from the experiences of others who may have similar stories. Each form of therapy offers a different dynamic and expectations. Finding the right one or combination can be challenging, but keep trying.

Individual counseling can help you change within your marriage. As you grow more independent and centered, you bring a new energy to the relationship, which often improves the communication between you and your spouse. If you can look at all the factors in your life that contribute to your personal unhappiness, you may realize you have choices to make about your personal and professional life that may allow for more fulfillment, which you would bring back to your relationship and help it evolve. Sometimes, when divorce is finally discussed as a possibility, that honest conversation becomes a pivotal factor that makes you and your spouse realize how unhappy you are and how necessary it is to make changes in the relationship.

In **marital counseling,** you could try to build a new relationship with your spouse based on who you both are now and what you choose to create together—from this point forward. If your spouse won't go with you for help, you can go alone for individual work.

You might **join a group** where you can find camaraderie and support to help you process your feelings and clarify your thinking. If addiction is part of your relationship, participation in your own 12-Step group will be invaluable. The more you focus on your own growth and healing, the better you will become at communicating from your highest and best SELF.

Postnuptial Agreement

A postnuptial agreement is a voluntary marriage contract that is created between spouses after their wedding. It can also be referred to as a "post-marriage agreement," a "mid-marriage agreement," or a "post-marital agreement." These agreements can be helpful in any marriage if the financial status of either you or your spouse has changed since you got married, or if you've changed careers, received an inheritance, sold a business, or experienced a change in investment income. You might want to consider this document, which could resolve your differences without the need for a separation or a divorce. A post-nuptial agreement can spell out the terms if a separation or divorce is decided upon in the future.

A postnuptial agreement can help you resolve issues in your marriage by fostering a meeting of the minds regarding parenting, chores, finances, assets, budgeting. You agree on what would happen should you divorce without having to actually create a divorce. The honest conversations you'd need to have to make your decisions would be easier once you've learned the Five Steps, the Miracle of Empathy, and how to communicate from your highest and best SELF.

Three criteria must be met to determine the validity of a postnuptial agreement:

- Full disclosure of all assets
- No duress in the creation of the agreement
- Fairness to both parties

Each of you must have your own legal counsel before signing a Postnuptial Agreement as it becomes a binding legal document should you decide to separate or get divorced in the future. Check to see if a Postnuptial Agreement is an option in your area by contacting an attorney should you choose to pursue this option.

Separation as an Option

If one or both of you is not able to "get to SELF" or is too triggered in your current situation, you may need to discuss a **separation for a limited time**. You can separate without the need for any legal discussions. If you have children, you can decide between yourselves whether one of you will move out for a period of time, or you can "nest" —in which case you can each come and go at designated times to be with the children who'll stay in the home. There are many subjects to cover if you will not be living together for any amount of time. Doing your best to create SELF-led decisions together will help maintain the peace and collaboration as much as possible. Some of the issues you will need to discuss include:

- Financial responsibilities
- Whether you'll come for continued counseling or mediation
- What to tell your children and others
- Whether dating is planned
- Whether one of you will move out for a period of time
- Any other issue that could affect the other

Legal Separation

If you decide to have a **legal separation,** you will need to consult an attorney at some point, because a legal document needs to be prepared and signed in court. A legal separation is like a divorce except for some differences, including:

- You can stay on each other's insurance policies—health, car, home.
- You cannot get married to someone else.

If Divorce is Your Decision

In the past, divorce has created turmoil, pain, financial disaster and broken families. It doesn't need to be that way. With Compassionate Mediation, healing can happen—and new, healthy relationships are possible. Here's the experience of one of my clients:

> "My (former) husband and I owned a restaurant together and worked together every day. We wanted to dissolve our marriage but not lose our business in the process. Linda helped us sort out the dysfunctional aspects of the relationship from the ways that we related that still worked and we wanted to retain, allowing us to continue to work together, successfully, for years.

> "She helped us separate from each other in a mutually respectable way so that I could move past my anger and disappointment in the failed relationship. She also helped us stay focused on what was really important, our 3-year-old child, making him the center of most of our decisions, and asking ourselves what was best for him as we wrote our joint parenting agreement.

> "When our son attended a group for kids of divorced parents at his school, they thought he was fantasizing when he told the counselor his parents worked together every day. Not only was Linda able to guide and advise us mindfully through the psychological and physical impact of divorce, but also the legal aspects—helping us write our divorce

decree to suit our needs, versus our lawyers'
sometimes petty and expensive suggestions."

This is just one example of the kind of positive, healing outcome that Compassionate Mediation can offer you.

Do You Know What You Truly Want?

As you proceed towards decisions for your future, it's imperative to get clear on what you want. Do you know what you want? Do you have an idea of what you need? Knowing what you want and need is always important, and even more so when making a life-changing decision. Are you ready to make your own choices, or are you trying to figure out what your partner wants, then reacting to what you think that is?

Unfortunately, many couples come to see me long after their troubles begin. I meet with each of them alone for a few minutes so that I can get a sense of how they have coped with their situation in the past. I also try to find out what they truly *want* to do, not their *reactions* to feeling hurt, sad, and unloved.

When I meet with a couple for the first time, I notice body language. I look at where you sit in the room (near your partner or at opposite sides of the sofa). I subtly decide which of you is more calm or more upset. I am curious as to who wants to separate or divorce, who wants to reconcile or create something new together.

I answer your questions about mediation, or give an initial overview of the process. I ask basic questions to get to know you both so that you each feel more comfortable with me. I ask when did you get married, how many children and how old, etc. I do my best to put you both at ease as much as possible.

I'll speak with you together for a few minutes and then ask to talk with each of you alone. As soon as the door closes, in many cases when one party is alone with me, there is a shift in his or her body language. Often tears flow as she puts down her protective walls to allow herself to feel the fear, sadness, and vulnerability underneath their defensive or angry Parts.

Often, one member of a couple is set on divorce and the other doesn't want one. If one of you wants a divorce and the other does not, the spouse who wants the divorce (Initiator) can slow the process enough to let the other partner (Non-Initiator) process his feelings. The more reluctant party has time to realize that a divorce is probably imminent and as he copes with his feelings about the loss, he can also begin to see what an independent future would look like. You can use this time to learn a new way to communicate and to talk about all the issues that have led to a conflict.

I ask the following questions to help us determine the conflicts and issues that have caused the problems in your relationship. You can answer these questions now and learn a great deal about yourself, your partner and your relationship.

If you had a magic wand, what would you want to have happen between you and your spouse in the future?

Your answer helps you set your *personal intention* for your relationship right now. Are you hoping your spouse will change to meet your needs? Are you reacting to his indifference thinking a divorce would set you free? Have you become attracted to someone else and want to explore single life? Do one or both of you secretly hope for a reconciliation? If so, we can build on that hope.

Your answers will help you get an idea of what you each want in this moment. How much do you each know about separation or divorce? Have you or your spouse already spoken with an attorney? Are your expectations realistic? Have you thought about what you want to do about staying in your house, dividing assets, discussing maintenance, childcare and parenting?

Questions for Each of You

- Who wants a divorce? (Initiator)

- Who hopes to form a new marriage together? (Non-Initiator)

- Why do you think divorce is a good option?

- Have you had any individual or marital counseling?

- What are the issues that cause you to think of leaving your marriage?

- Why has divorce become an option? Is it a way to get your spouse's attention?

- Is there another person involved outside your relationship?

- Would counseling help to create a new relationship between you?

Who Wants the Divorce?

I want to know who is the Initiator and Non-initiator as different Parts are triggered in each. The Initiator is usually more emotionally ready for the process of divorce. The Initiator is also more prepared for the legal process as he or she has been dealing with the emotions of sadness and anger before having even brought up the subject of divorce. The other party may have been in denial about the problems or still hoping for a way to get beyond the current situation and go back to the love once shared in the past.

(For the following, please substitute him/her as needed.)

I tell the Initiator:
If You Want a Divorce...

"This process of Compassionate Mediation will help you facilitate a divorce if that is what you want to accomplish. The time we take will avoid conflict in the future, and give your partner a chance to catch up emotionally with where you are now. Also, if you just go and file for divorce now, your spouse can delay and stall the process in many different ways.

"If you give your spouse time to process his feelings and address his fears, you will avoid legal fees and maneuvering. Your spouse is less likely to sabotage the process, and you'll save time and money that it takes to have your lawyer pursue legal remedies that may or may not work. If you let me help you both talk about your feelings (along with financial and other issues), your spouse may realize that he is ready for the conversations he needs to have to begin a new life."

I tell the Non-Initiator:
If You Don't Want a Divorce...

"I know that you feel you are not ready to divorce, and want to try counseling first. If your spouse is too angry or resistant to therapy, you'll be wasting your time, and your spouse won't stay for that process. On the other hand, if you are willing to talk about a possibility of a separation or a divorce and engage in a discussion of what that could look like, your spouse may realize that counseling would be a better option than ending your marriage right now.

"Otherwise, your spouse will likely hire an attorney and file for divorce to make sure that you know he is serious. Then you will have 30 days to find an attorney and file a response. The court will then be involved with status calls and legal maneuvers and you may not have any chance for discussion beyond that without attorneys involved. Right now your spouse is not emotionally available for marriage counseling. Maybe he needs to explore what a separation or divorce would look like before he can commit to working on the marriage. If I can help you feel safe enough to know that you won't have to decide

or sign anything without a lawyer helping you in the future, you can at least show up for the conversation and keep a dialogue possible.

"And HOW you show up will determine your partner's willingness to consider counseling in the future. If you are open and compassionate, you have a better chance of convincing your partner that you can change and a new relationship with you would meet his needs. At the same time, you will both learn a new method of communication that will heal the past and give you tools for a more loving and empathetic relationship in the future.

"Sometimes an individual needs to see the reality of what a divorce would look like before being able to commit to working on the marriage. If I can help you listen with compassion to your partner's reasons for wanting to end your marriage, she may feel more heard and understood than they have in the past. She could change her desire to end the marriage. If she experiences you as more calm, compassionate, and empathetic (i.e. more in SELF) then she may come to believe a new relationship IS possible with you."

What are the Reasons You're Thinking about Divorce?

When I listen for the reasons one or both of you have thought about a divorce, I try to see if either party has any desire to stay together to create a new and different relationship. Often one or both of you may be resigned to the decision of the other, not realizing you have other options to be considered.

If you learn Compassionate Communication, you can discuss all your long-standing issues with mutual respect and confidence. Your new skills of listening with empathy and asking for what you want and need help create a fertile ground for building something new.

Even if a third party is now involved in an emotional or physical affair, you can still heal from that betrayal and move forward with optimism and possibility. However, if there is adultery, abuse, or addiction without a desire to stop or change the behavior, then divorce will be the most likely outcome.

However, if there are hurt feelings that have never been acknowledged or healed, there is a chance that communications training can finally enable you and your spouse to feel seen, heard, and acknowledged. I talk with each of you individually and find out all I can about your desires, unmet needs and expectations, hopes and dreams.

What are your most important issues right now?

- *What are your biggest concerns (money, children, loneliness, health)?*

- *Is there any fear of physical abuse?*

- *Is either one of you having an affair?*

- *How contentious is the living arrangement?*

- *How are your children doing?*

- *What are the ages of your children?*

- *How much do the children know about your current relationship?*

- *Do we need to discuss the children in the first session?*

- *What do you each want to share with your children?*

- *When do you each want to talk with the children?*

- *What do you want to tell other people and when?*

- *What needs to happen until the next session?*

I ask these questions to see what is the most pressing need to be covered in this first session. The goal is to create a sense of peace and safety in your home from this moment on as you explore all your options for your future.

Chapter 6
Learn Your Rights

*"Every time you are tempted to react in the same old way
ask if you want to be a prisoner of the past
or a pioneer of the future.'*
—Deepak Chopra, Author

Being present, in the moment, is a choice, and as Deepak Chopra has noted, "When you make a choice, you change the future." Compassionate Mediation gives you an opportunity to make choices in this moment to create a new relationship from your highest and best SELF.

Many couples begin a conversation about divorce with little or no prior discussion of issues that one or both of them may have ignored or taken for granted. Perhaps you are more responsible for paying bills than your spouse, and you wish that your partner were more pro-active and involved. You may not share equal knowledge of what you both currently earn, spend and save. You may have never discussed retirement plans, savings for your children's college costs, or how discretionary income can be spent.

All of these topics are on the table when divorce is planned, but it is also paramount that they be part of a healthy relationship in which both parties are equal and informed partners.

In many situations, each member of the couple has taken on the same roles of their parents, and then come to resent the fact that the other spouse doesn't earn more, parent more or pay more attention to the financial and parental details in their lives.

When intimacy is an issue, as it often is, it's due to the resentments, judgments, and blame that create walls and filters that have inhibited or blocked their sex lives. Couples can live separately and separated under the same roof for years, and even decades. If they took the time to heal the pain, forgive, and be grateful for what they do share, they could renew the bond that brought them together years before.

Learning how to talk compassionately about all subjects creates a sense of safety and trust that probably has been missing for a long time. You can make the time for all these conversations and give you and your spouse, and your family, an opportunity for an intimate and compassionate new beginning.

However, if you or your spouse has ever thought about a separation or divorce, it may be necessary to explore what those possibilities would entail. You would each feel more informed and empowered to create a new relationship together having discussed the following issues with compassion and courage.

Important Information for Discussion

The following information is just a partial overview of the types of conversations you and your spouse can begin. The laws will vary in each state and country. This is meant to introduce these concepts to you and not to offer legal advice. Be sure to consult with an attorney if you choose to go forward with any legal document.

Property Settlement, Maintenance, Parenting/Child Support

In Compassionate Mediation, you'll discuss all the issues that come up when considering a legal separation or divorce. These subjects focus on the respective rights and responsibilities of each party. If you proceed to a divorce, you'll both need legal counsel at some point, but you begin the discussion together without the need for attorneys. You can work out the details together for all decisions that need to be made at this time.

You will review the following:

- Property Division
- Maintenance (or Alimony) Allocation
- Child Support and Parenting Issues

Property Settlements

The division of property will vary depending on the laws of the area in which you live. Where **community property** is the standard, the division is likely to be a fifty-fifty split. In other areas, the decision on how to divide assets is based on **Equitable Distribution** and **Relevant Criteria.**

Of course, what is "equitable" to one party may not feel fair to the other, so there is a set of "relevant criteria" for property division that serve as guidelines should a judge be deciding the outcome of the case. Among the criteria that may be considered are the respective income of each party, the length of the marriage, and the health and income earning potential of each, among other factors.

In determining the division of property, *the contribution of a spouse as homemaker is often held to be as valuable as the income earned by the other spouse.* Other relevant factors include where the children will reside, the age and health of each spouse, and how much maintenance or alimony will possibly be paid.

The property to be divided is called the **marital estate** and may include the value of your and your spouse's home, investments, bank accounts, stock and bond accounts, retirement accounts (e.g., pensions, IRAs, 401Ks), businesses that may be owned, cars, cash value of any life insurance policies, and all money earned and all property acquired during the course of the marriage, no matter whose name is listed as owner.

Some assets aren't included in the marital estate. These are referred to as **non-marital assets,** and may include premarital assets, (those you had before you were married,) any assets acquired by gift or inheritance provided that only one spouse's name is on the asset(s), and the asset(s) was never commingled.

Inherited assets are considered commingled when both spouses are listed as owners, or if ever one spouse took some of an inherited asset and used it for a joint marital expense. For example, if one spouse took out $10,000 to buy stocks in both spouses' names and then put that $10,000 back into the inheritance ledger, it might be considered commingled.

As you are accumulating and sharing information about all of your assets, you will also share data about your debts.

Debts

Debts may also be marital, even if only one spouse incurred them. Debts are also divided on an equitable basis and it must be decided who's responsible for paying which debt. There may also be non-marital debts. As you discuss both assets and debts, you will each become fully informed.

Decisions About Your Other Assets

When you begin to think of dividing the assets, you'll need to make some decisions about the **marital home**. Often, this is one of the most emotional issues of the divorce process, and when the discussion begins about "breaking up the home," many couples do consider working harder to create a new marriage to keep the family intact. So it's a good idea to take your time to consider all the options for your future.

That said, staying together "for the sake of the children" is only a good idea when you and your spouse can create a healthy relationship that you would like your children to emulate someday. Otherwise, they see your stress and resentment as a model for marriage that is not in anyone's best interest.

When discussing possible scenarios, keep your mind open. You can decide to sell the house and divide the net proceeds. You can choose to let one parent live there with the children for a certain amount of time, with the house to be sold and the sale price split at the end of a designated time-period. You can discuss all of your options in mediation.

Retirement funds may also be marital assets that can be divided, no matter whose name is on the retirement account. Keep in mind that some portion of the accounts may have been accumulated before the marriage and may be deemed "non-marital."

When a **business** is a marital asset, you may need to hire an expert to put a value on the business. You and your spouse can possibly agree on one expert and then use the valuation as a basis for asset division.

Term life insurance isn't considered a marital asset. However, if you have a **whole life insurance policy**, there may be a cash value that is a marital asset. A life insurance policy may be used to guarantee the amount of maintenance or child support to be paid after the divorce.

There are many details and pieces of information that will change depending on where you live and what the law allows.

As you gather all the information needed, you may be:

- Confused by all the details

- Overwhelmed by all that needs to be done

- Surprised by how much (or how little) you have acquired in your life together

- Hurt, sad, or angry that you haven't been informed earlier

- Guilty, ashamed, or self-critical for ignoring this for so long

- Empowered to offer your opinion and your needs

- Worried about your future

Whatever your initial response, you now have an awareness of the financial information you need to decide your future. Once you have gathered all this information, you can use this knowledge to create a new relationship in which you feel respected and heard, which could begin to make all the difference you need to feel safe and happy again.

What You Can Do Starting Now

Make a list of all your assets and debts. Discuss where you can locate the information so that you both feel equally informed and empowered. You can gather all your financial data and sit down with your partner to share your feelings and thoughts about future budgeting, cash flow, and disposable income. You can compare your visions for college funding, retirement planning, and vacation ideas.

You will need to talk about all of these topics if you choose to get divorced. Often a divorce causes a financial strain that forces you both to spend less money or earn more money. Try to focus on your spending in your current relationship and see if that effort lessens stress and resentment as you both move in the direction of complaining less and contributing more. Talk about all of your issues in the context of a future, improved relationship, and see how that feels to each and both of you.

As you both offer input and support to each other, you may find resentments diminish and a newfound feeling of togetherness replaces the isolation one or both of you may have experienced. You may feel this is the first time you are acknowledged to be an equal partner, or the first time you feel heard and understood and supported.

You will need to talk about all of these topics if you choose to get divorced. Often a divorce causes a financial strain that forces you both to spend less money or earn more money. Try to focus on your spending in your current relationship and see if that effort lessens stress and resentment as you both move in the direction of complaining less and contributing more. Talk about all of your issues in the context of a future, improved relationship, and see how that feels to each and both of you.

If you eventually decide to separate or divorce, all of these discussions will make that process easier to complete. You will have practiced a SELF-led discussion of important topics that will help you feel informed and empowered to make healthy choices in the future.

Assets and Debts

You can begin by making a list of what you do know, and what you don't know. Then you can ask your spouse to fill in the missing details and show you how to access all the information that is relevant to your growing financial awareness.

As you and your partner share the details, you also have the opportunity to share hopes and dreams for the future. Taking the time you need in Compassionate Mediation to explore the emotional, financial, and legal issues will give you the power to make mindful, conscious, empowered choices in the future.

Some of the information to share includes:

- Income: yours and your spouse's income (including bonuses)
- Expenses: daily, weekly, monthly, yearly
- Assets: Marital and non-marital
  - Cash in checking accounts and savings accounts
  - Real estate: (may need current appraisals)
    - Your marital home
    - Other real estate you own
  - Retirement Funds: 401Ks, SEP Accounts, IRAs (Traditional and Roth)
  - Pension Information
  - Life Insurance (cash value)
  - Investment portfolio: stocks, bonds, certificates of deposit
  - Personal property:
    - Cars, boats, motorcycles, vehicles
    - Furnishings, furniture
    - Jewelry
  - Ownership in businesses
- Debts: Marital and Non-Marital
  - Home mortgage or home equity loans
  - Car loans
  - Credit cards
  - Student loans

The division of assets, or Property Division, is only one aspect of the current and future financial discussions that you'll need to share. If you are considering the possibility of a separation or divorce, maintenance will become another issue for decision-making.

Maintenance (or Alimony)

"Maintenance" is the term that was previously referred to as alimony. If one party receives maintenance, the amount and length of time is based on many factors, including the need of that spouse and the other spouse's ability to pay. Some states now have guidelines for maintenance based on the length of the marriage and percentages of the respective incomes of both parties. Maintenance is taxable to the recipient.

The amount of maintenance will vary, as will the length of time it's paid. If two spouses have equal earnings, there may be no maintenance paid by either. In long-term marriages where one party has been out of the work force, the amount may be greater at first and then diminish as he or she has more experience in becoming self-supporting. There are cases in which a higher-earning wife pays maintenance to her husband.

Maintenance can be **reviewable, modifiable, or permanent**. In the future, the court may terminate, amend, or modify the maintenance amount.

Modifiable maintenance means that if the circumstances of either spouse change, they can ask to have the maintenance amount reviewed. **Permanent maintenance** is sometimes granted. It may pertain to marriages in which the spouse receiving maintenance has been out of the work force for a long time and may have some health issues that would prevent him or her from being able to earn money in the future. Some states are now changing their statutes to provide permanent maintenance in various circumstances. Go online and check the laws in your state or make an appointment with an attorney to learn your rights in your area.

Maintenance is based on how much is earned and how much is spent by each party. You'll have to create a **budget** that reflects the current amount spent each month for the household. Often couples are oblivious to how much money goes out each month, and are very surprised when the costs are totaled. Sometimes this one exercise is enough to change the spending habits of one or both parties, which alleviates some of the financial strain and a lot of the resentment from the other spouse. As you have the conversation about the possibility of maintenance, you may be motivated to pay more attention to your current and future decisions.

Starting Now

Take the time to fill out a budget for your current expenses. It will be valuable, I promise you. Learn how much it costs to support your family and notice where the funds are going on a weekly, monthly, and yearly basis. You will be amazed at how much everything costs. You will have more compassion for the wage earner(s) and more understanding of the concerns. You can begin a dialogue that will allow you each to have a say in how you spend your money in the future. You will have to create a budget if you get divorced, so why not try it while you are still married and see the changes that can happen as a result of feeling like an equal, valuable and respected partner?

You can use the following budget form to begin. If you'd like a clean copy, please visit LindaKroll.com/book-resources.

MONTHLY BUDGET OF EXPENSES

HOUSING

Rent _____

Mortgage _____

Second Mortgage (Home Equity Loans) _____

Real Estate Tax _____

Homeowners/Renters' Insurance _____

Other (itemize below) _____

                                    Subtotal _____

UTILITIES

Electricity _____

Gas/Oil _____

Telephone _____

Water _____

Cable TV _____

Internet Access _____

Other (itemize below) _____

                                    Subtotal _____

HOUSEHOLD OPERATION/MAINTENANCE

Repairs (normal/ongoing) _____

Appliance Service Contracts _____

Garden and Yard Work _____

Domestic Help _____

Other (itemize below) _____

                                    Subtotal _____

FOOD _____

CLOTHING _____

                            PAGE 1 TOTAL _____

TRANSPORTATION

Gasoline _____

Auto repair and maintenance _____

Auto license and stickers _____

Auto insurance (monthly average) _____

Auto installments or lease amounts _____

Other (bus, taxi, parking, etc.) _____

Subtotal _____

HEALTH

Medical/hospital insurance _____

Dental insurance _____

Medical/healthcare (not covered) _____

Dental care (not covered) _____

Medicine _____

Life/Disability insurance
(list policies and premiums below) _____

Subtotal _____

CHILDREN'S EDUCATION/CHILDCARE

Children's day care _____

Private school tuition _____

College tuition (only if current) _____

Room and board _____

Books and fees _____

Sports, Music Lessons, Tutoring _____

Children's allowance _____

Other _____

Subtotal _____

PAGE 2 TOTAL _____

EDUCATION

Tuition   _____

Books and fees   _____

Other (itemize below)   _____

                Subtotal   _____

PERSONAL/ENTERTAINMENT EXPENSES

Drug/Variety store items   _____

Books, magazines, newspapers   _____

Dry cleaning and laundry   _____

Haircuts/coloring   _____

Dues (club/professional not listed as
business expenses)   _____

Charities, contributions   _____

Cultural/Recreational (itemize below)   _____

Other (itemize below)   _____

          Subtotal   _____

VACATION

Self   _____

Children   _____

Summer camp   _____

          Subtotal   _____

GIFTS (holidays and birthdays)   _____

SAVINGS   _____
DEBT PAYMENT (not listed above)   _____

RETIREMENT ACCOUNTS   _____

          PAGE 3 TOTAL   _____

          GRAND TOTAL   _____

SELF-Led Conversations

In the conversations you have about how your marriage could end, you will also have a plan for a new beginning based on full disclosure of all important financial realities, expectations, needs, and desires. Again, have a heart-to-heart discussion about how you feel regarding spending habits and purchases. What mutually satisfying decisions can you both make when you come from your highest and best SELF, without the walls that kept you feeling angry and withdrawn? You might be surprised at how well you can maneuver these issues when you are both trying to understand and empathize instead of defend or attack.

As you go over your budget form together, you may find that you have more in common than you realize. Looking at your current spending habits can inspire you to make changes which your partner has been seeking for years. Also, as you realize the cost of keeping one household working, you realize that there isn't enough money to support two households, which might motivate you to try harder to resolve your differences and keep your family and finances intact.

Compassionate Mediation focuses on finances and legal rights and responsibilities, and it is also a forum for your discussions about parenting styles, duties, and ideology. It helps you create a more dynamic partnership moving forward in a new and better marriage, and it is a way to talk about all these subjects should you choose to dissolve your union.

Parenting and Child Support

When you consider a potential separation or divorce, you need to come to agreement about your children and their care. If you decide to separate informally, then Compassionate Mediation can lead you through the steps to take. You'll create a schedule that meets your needs and the needs of your children. You will decide how you will handle finances and costs of caring for the children. You can talk about what you'll say to your children and to others (see Chapter 12).

If you decide to change your relationship legally, then a legal document may include the following considerations. When making decisions about parenting time and child support payments, a divorce decree requires a "custody designation." The options are sole or joint legal custody and sole or joint physical custody.

Usually, **joint legal custody** means that both parents will have a voice in their children's medical and educational decisions. **Joint physical custody** means the children will live with both parents at least some of the time. Often the designation is joint legal custody and joint physical custody with one parent's home as the **primary residence**.

The non-residential or non-custodial parent often pays child support until each child reaches the age of 18 or graduates high school, whichever is later. The amount of child support to be paid is determined by the number of children and the net income of the payor. Each state has its own statutes that cover the details of the amounts owed. However, the courts may deviate from these percentages based on the facts of each situation. Child support is usually tax-free to the recipient.

A **Parenting Agreement** creates a baseline of decisions. In my mediated documents, I often create a "shared parenting agreement" that doesn't designate one "residential" parent, but allows for an equitable distribution of time with the children and financial contributions by each parent.

As long as the two of you can agree to co-parent in the best interests of your children, you can be flexible. You can work out a parenting schedule based on the needs of your children and each parent's availability. The more you and your partner each relate from SELF, the more connection you will maintain as you discuss difficult subjects. You can confidently work together to reach agreements.

If a legal separation or divorce occurs, my favorite scenario is two loving homes where children feel comfortable. Each parent appreciates the need for both of them to be a positive influence in their children's lives.

Some of the other issues that come up depend on the ages and maturity of your children. The residence of the children can change every other week, different days during the week, alternate weekends and one night a week, or any other scenario that you both decide.

You'll also need to specify who pays for extra expenses, which may include camp, lessons, tutors, and childcare. One parent may cover insurance for the children, and the other parent may contribute to extraordinary medical expenses, such as orthodontia or counseling.

The parenting discussion is often the most emotional, and the one area where both parties are the most conflicted. Leaving a child or children is the last wish of any parent, and facing that possibility can be very motivating for healing instead of leaving.

The Parenting Agreement should be reviewed at least once a year to make sure it's meeting everyone's needs as much as possible.

Whatever your reason for considering divorce, if you whole-heartedly put your efforts into creating a SELF-led relationship with your spouse, your family can stay intact or become *re-structured* in a kind and peaceful process.

Your Personal Research

As you consider divorce, you should begin to do research on what it would cost to live on your own. You may want to explore other places where you could live and how much that would cost monthly. You will definitely need to investigate options for health insurance for yourself: you may qualify for COBRA coverage on your spouse's health insurance policy, but that often only lasts for 36 (thirty-six) months and then you'll need your own policy.

Aside from the financial research, take the time you need to heal your heart, forgive yourself and your spouse, and then decide what comes next. You can pursue a Compassionate Relationship for a time, and put off the discussion of divorce as you and your spouse give a full-fledged effort to practice the skills of Compassionate Communication. You will heal burdens from your past, let go of limiting beliefs (and judgments, walls and filters), connect to your spiritual source and relate to each other from your highest and best SELF.

You can practice exquisite SELF-care (see Section Three) and forgive yourself and your partner, as you stay grateful for all you do share, and become willing to focus on and augment the love you once felt for each other.

Choosing an Attorney

Who will serve as your legal counsel is an important decision. You should interview several until you find one with whom you feel comfortable. Remember, *you're* hiring the attorney and he or she is working *for you.* You'll want someone with whom you can collaborate on reaching a settlement, and who's open to working with mediators and negotiating in good faith with your spouse's attorney.

Fees and retainers for attorneys differ between attorneys as well as time spent on your case, whether in their office, court, or trial. Court costs are often separate. You should receive copies of all filings and correspondences. There will be a contract to sign. Many will send itemized bills each month, but you may have to request these. You should expect your attorney to return phone calls within twenty-four hours or to have someone in his or her office return your call during that time.

Some attorneys don't charge for very short phone calls, while others bill for fifteen minutes no matter how brief the conversation. Ask your attorney if you will be billed for six-, ten- or fifteen-minute increments, and then use your time efficiently.

Timing Issues if Legal Papers are Served

At any time, your spouse may decide to file for divorce, and let you know in person or by having you handed the divorce papers by someone else.

If you're served legal divorce papers, you should consult an attorney *immediately*. You'll have a specified time, usually 30 (thirty) days, in which to file a legal response in court. Failure to respond within the required time may result in legal sanctions against you by the court, or you could be considered in default. If you default, your spouse could proceed with the divorce without your knowledge, and obtain a divorce and property division in which you don't participate. **So, again, if your spouse ever serves you papers, you should consult an attorney *immediately*. Otherwise, take your time.**

Take Your Time

A divorce requires many decisions, which is why you need to take your time and proceed at a pace that's comfortable for you. Aside from the legal and financial decisions, you have to take care of yourself emotionally. Take all the time you need to make any decision, and then take more time to adjust emotionally as you move along through the process. Sometimes, it takes years to decide to get to the point of filing for divorce and more years to actually finalize it.

Whether you're beginning to think about the possibility of divorce or your spouse has recently served you with papers, *take the time you need* to prepare yourself mentally, emotionally, legally, and financially.

Some deadlines are built into the process. If you have court dates, for instance, you must comply, although continuances are often granted for a variety of reasons. **In mediation, you can set your own timing.**

Unless there's a compelling and non-modifiable deadline for something, learn to listen to your own internal voice and honor it, and disregard others who tell you to hurry the process. They're often well-meaning friends or relatives who think that as soon as the divorce is over, you can simply "move on." But you "move on" as the divorce proceeds, and sometimes, you're just not ready to let go until you've done some of the necessary personal work that only time helps you accomplish.

So don't criticize yourself for not getting enough done, or taking time off, or not wanting to think about it or deal with it. That's part of the process. Your inner voice will tell you *when* you're ready to engage. You can't hide under the covers forever—though at times that feels like the most-inviting scenario. But you can try to be as much in control of the time frame as feels comfortable for you, no matter what your spouse, lawyer, or anyone else says. And be careful when you are driving, since people are prone to have more automobile accidents when considering a divorce or going through one.

The Importance of Taking Your Time with Awareness.

Pauline was in a support group because her husband was having an affair and wanted a divorce. She decided that she was going to continue to be extremely reliable and efficient as ever, and proceeded to organize every aspect of the divorce. She got the necessary house appraisals, she put together all the needed financial information, and she did all that she could do to comply with her husband's deadlines.

Each time Pauline spoke in the group, everyone was amazed at the equanimity she maintained throughout the months until the divorce was final, and her husband married his girlfriend. Several months later, Pauline was in another support group, and each week she cried more and became increasingly depressed. She wished she had taken more time to adjust emotionally so that she could have become empowered by her anger and not been so amenable to everything her husband wanted her to do.

That's one client's story. Here's another's.

Carol never joined a group because she was separated for nine years before her divorce became final. She told herself that she needed to stay married legally "for the sake of her children." On one hand, she maintained the security of being connected to her husband's income potential. On the other hand, his wealth was highest in Year Seven, and by the time the divorce was final, he had lost a great deal of money. And furthermore when she finally did decide to get divorced, she learned that her children wished it had been over years before.

There are many different timing scenarios that can be played out, but the one that works for you is personal *to you.* Be honest with yourself about whether you are denying, procrastinating, hiding out, recuperating, healing, or preparing.

This is a time to join a support group, see a counselor, and to find ways to take care of your personal feelings and needs. You might begin to journal or learn how to meditate. There are good books to read to help foster your personal and spiritual growth. Remember to breathe. Taking deep breaths, so that you fill yourself with oxygen, helps you to relax and calm yourself.

One important caveat to "taking your time" is this: Make sure you aren't stalling out of denial or some illusory hope that if you hang in there long enough "you will change your spouse." *There's nothing you can say or do that will change someone else.* Each person has to make his or her own decision—it's the only way to grow.

Your own power lies in your ability to change yourself. Take the time you need to exercise your power in a way that's healthy for you and your children. Take the time you need to go into marital counseling if your spouse agrees and if you think it might help heal the issues that are leading to divorce. *Take the time you need* to prepare emotionally for each new stage of a separation or divorce.

Don't waste your energy trying to *make someone else change*. As Byron Katie said, *"Thinking that people should do or be anything but what they are is like saying the tree over there should be the sky."* Don't keep turning the other cheek to abuse of any kind. Change yourself and no matter what happens, I promise, you'll be happier, healthier, and feel more alive and energized than you ever may have dreamed.

Make Your SELF-Led Decision

The process of Compassionate Mediation offers you the skills to communicate your needs and desires as you listen with empathy to your partner. You can then decide if you want to stay together and focus on creating a new and better relationship or move in the direction of a separation or SELF-Led Divorce. Whatever you decide, you'll be able to discuss it with respect and consideration.

As you decide what to do next, you will be able to take better care of yourself and minimize your stress at this difficult time. You can *change your pattern of thinking* about your partner and your situation and choose thoughts that are more aligned with SELF-care and SELF-love, as well as compassion for your partner.

As Lissa Rankin wrote in her book, *Mind Over Medicine,* *"As far as your body's health is concerned,* **thoughts, beliefs, and** **feelings** [emphasis added] *that trigger the stress response may damage your health more than a poor diet, avoiding exercise, bad habits, and sleep deprivation. But the good news is that the opposite is also true!* **Because your thoughts, beliefs, and feelings are at** **least partially under your control, you have the power to** **switch off your body's stress responses** [emphasis added] *and return the nervous system to the health-inducing relaxation response that activates the body's natural self repair."*

Changing your thoughts, healing your past, and unburdening your Inner Child will help you reduce stress. The next section has other techniques you can use starting now.

SECTION THREE
Reduce Your Stress with Exquisite SELF Care

Chapter 7
Tune In To Your SELF

"Meditation is about love and loving life.
When you cultivate this love,
it gives you clarity and compassion for life,
and your actions happen in accordance with that."
—Jon Kabat-Zinn, Author

Taking care of yourself is vitally important. If you have had conflict in your relationship, you have been experiencing a lot of stress. Sometimes, you might think that a divorce would help to lessen your stress. You might think that you will solve your problems by ending your relationship. Instead of working through the issues that cause you stress, you or your partner may feel that leaving is the only way to end the suffering.

It doesn't have to be that way. The process of divorce— or even thinking about the possibility of a divorce—can cause more stress than taking the time to heal the problems that caused the stress in the first place.

If you take a moment and imagine that you are in conflict with your partner, do you feel what happens in your body? Do you constrict, tighten, get agitated? You might feel it in your stomach, your chest, your shoulders, your jaw. You might get a headache. When your body reacts to stress, you armor yourself internally for what may feel like danger. All the thoughts that you think when you judge your partner create the same kinds of stress reactions in your body.

Take a moment and just witness these internal physiological reactions. Don't judge them or try to change them. Just accept the fact that stress, or even a thought about someone or something, can trigger some bodily responses that cause you distress.

As you practice Compassionate Communication along with exquisite SELF-care, you have more energy and patience to deal with your problems in productive, pro-active ways. You don't need to put those walls around your heart to try to protect yourself, and you can forge a new beginning with your partner.

When even one partner is "in SELF", the energy of the discussion can shift from anger and resentment to respectful dialogue about individual desires and needs. A positive outcome is easier when both parties are working towards a peaceful resolution instead of arguing to make the other person wrong. As my dear friends and mentors SARK and Dr. John Waddell say in their book, *Succulent Wild Love*, *"A Joyful Solution is an agreement that everyone is enthusiastic about keeping."* The more you are SELF-led, the more peace, love and joy you will experience.

As conflict diminishes, so does stress. Even if you decide to end your marriage, Compassionate Communication and Compassionate Mediation provide an opportunity for you to forgive yourself and your spouse so that the future is free from past wounds or old walls. You will experience more peace within your relationship and more inner peace as well.

In his new book *destressifying*, davidji says *"Don't think I'm getting all 'woo woo' on you. We all want to live lives of greater peace in a world filled with peace."* I don't want you to think I'm too *woo woo* either, although some of the following information might seem that way. But it is important to know that you can focus on getting to SELF and reducing your stress with mediation, yoga, breath work, and making healthy choices that increase SELF-presence and energy. From a more expanded state of SELF-Leadership, rather than the constricted view of your reactive Parts, you can create a calm and peaceful forum for Compassionate Communication. Minimizing your stress is the fastest way to reach your best possible outcome.

Stress—Fight or Flight (or Freeze)

The "fight/flight" response (or "fight/flight/freeze response") is *"a physiological reaction that occurs in response to a perceived harmful event, attack, or threat to survival."* This primitive "fight/flight response" still remains in your brain, and you still experience it when faced with stressful situations today. Perhaps you are engaged in active battles at home—with your children as silent witnesses—as you barrage each other with anger and resentment. Or you have become walled and withholding, modeling for your children a relationship devoid of affection and intimacy.

Your body may be in constant alert mode because you are thinking thoughts that trigger a reaction telling you that you are not safe. There are techniques you can learn to make different choices in how you respond.

When you are stressed with relationship issues, or facing the possibility of a separation or divorce, it is easy to feel overwhelmed, depleted and exhausted. You may be experiencing more anxiety, insomnia, or difficulty focusing on your daily responsibilities. You may find that you are more irritable or compulsive, or suffer from indigestion or an inflammatory condition. Or you might become lethargic, depressed, and losing or gaining weight.

What Causes You Stress

Make a list of what causes you stress. What is your partner doing that bothers you or triggers some automatic response? Various factors that create stress include:

- Not getting your needs met because of some obstacle
- Too many responsibilities for chores, finances, children
- No balance in life between sleep, fun, work, play
- Insufficient SELF-care
- Relationships with partners, friends, family, children, parents, co-workers
- Worry about how your choices will affect your future

Notice Your Energy Whenever You're Stressed

Notice your body and your energy whenever you're feeling stressed. As you become more conscious and aware, you will tune in to your body to see what messages it is giving you. Are you "uptight, anxious, in pain?" Do you clench your teeth at night? Are your shoulders sore? Do you feel tension in your neck or back? If you took the time to reduce your stress, you would feel better physically and emotionally.

Sometimes, when stressed, you might try to avoid the cause of the stress by staying busy, numbing out, or resorting to extreme behaviors to take your attention away from your feelings. However, your body has its own intelligence and is often more in tune with what you are experiencing than your mind will admit.

Whatever you are feeling in your body right now, just notice. Notice how you are feeling.

Now take a breath. A deep breath. Inhale so that your abdomen inflates like a balloon. Exhale so that your belly button returns back towards your spine. Do it again. Inhale, belly expands like a balloon. Exhale, belly button back towards your spine, Inhale. Exhale. Deep slow belly breaths. Breathe deeply 2 or 3 more times, and then let your breath return to normal. "Normal breathing" is what you do when you are not thinking about it.

Now notice your body. Is it calming down? Less constricted? Even *one breath* can reset your internal monologue, change the channel, give you a moment to think a new thought or make a more conscious choice in how you want to *respond* to something, rather than to *react* unconsciously.

When you "tune in" to yourself, you are paying attention, being mindful, staying present. You can tune in by focusing on your body, your breath, and your inner voice. With awareness and intention, you can quiet the constant chatter of your *egoic* mind and tune in to the deeper messages within your heart. Conscious breathing techniques, yoga postures, and a practice of meditation all enhance your ability to be "in SELF."

As you become more aware, conscious, SELF led, you begin to have different levels of reaction to your partner and your life. Instead of the primordial "fight-flight", or the more contemporary and socially acceptable reactive behaviors of "sarcasm" or "withholding," you learn how to respond with "spontaneously correct choices," born of your SELF at that moment, unfettered from reflexive rehashing of past pain.

In SELF you intuitively know there are more creative ways to handle conflict than the ones you have used in the past. You recognize that you can partner in resolving the issues from a SELF led perspective that brings more calm, clarity, compassion, and connection to the process.

Meditation Can Reverse the Effects of Stress

Meditation is a practice of restful awareness. The benefits of meditation—reducing stress, increasing immune functioning, increasing sexual hormones, maintaining calm in the middle of difficult situations, not attaching to or believing all your thoughts—help to create a new paradigm for conflict resolution. Deepak Chopra has said *"Meditation is not a way of making your mind quiet. It's a way of entering into the quiet that's already there, buried under the 50,000 thoughts the average person thinks every day."*

Imagine what it would be like to approach your partner from that quiet state, or "beginner's mind," where you show up with a clean slate and allow both of you to relate in the present moment. Give it a try and see changes occur before your eyes.

It has been medically proven that for many people, practicing meditation can reverse the effects of stress, inducing a state of "restful awareness" in which the following can occur:

- Heart rate slows down
- Blood pressure normalizes
- Breathing slows
- Adrenal glands and hormones normalize
- Platelet function normalizes
- Immune system grows stronger

Meditation lowers your stress level. You are more able to be "in SELF," and all your relationships improve. You can feel more vital, energized, rested, restored. You may find yourself feeling happier, more alive and creative, lighter and filled with joy.

How would you like to be handling your stress? How could you respond more from SELF? The sooner you can get to SELF, the calmer you'll be.

Meditation as a Spiritual Quest

When you meditate, you practice detaching from the conditioned thoughts and beliefs of your ego (and Family of Origin), and begin to "attune" to the innate desires of your SELF (or Soul.)

Meditation moves your response system from *reactive*—where you go into old "knee jerk" behaviors—and helps you to become more *reflective* and make conscious choices. You are able to break out of past conditioning of your Family of Origin and be willing to tap into the *unconditioned SELF* of your spiritual nature, which offers more compassion and connection.

The purpose of meditation can also be part of a spiritual quest to find out who you truly are and help you live your life more in SELF than in reactive Parts. Meditation takes you beyond your mind, intellect, and ego to your Soul and Spirit.

153

You remember who you can be and not who you have become defensively in your relationship. You learn how to bring the best version of your SELF to your partnership and then watch it miraculously begin to transform.

davidji, in his book *The Secrets of Meditation*, offers this observation: *"Over time, meditation quiets you to a state where you experience life with a deeper understanding of your true Self, which can open the door to spiritual exploration, connection, discovery and fulfillment. It is along the so-called spiritual path that you truly can experience your unbounded Self—your unconditioned Self—the infinite you that rests at the core of who you are underneath your body and beneath this worldly garb of title, roles, masks, ego and the complexities of this life."*

As you meditate, you connect with your essential SELF and look within to get your needs met. You can remember your fundamental wholeness, divinity, and perfection, and connect with your Spirit on a daily basis. You experience silence and relaxation, and enrich your active daily life and all your relationships.

In speaking of the benefits of meditation, Dick Schwartz said, *"This innate core within us is what some people call our Buddha nature, soul, 'atman,' and so forth. The problem is that too often this essence—what I call the Self—has been obscured by the protective parts of us that try to keep our lives on track in the mistaken belief that they know best. Thus, the process of coming to a fuller experience of self-compassion typically begins with creating open space for this Self to come forward."*

Meditation can help you remember that you are a reflection of the Divine, as is your partner. We're all one, and we're all divine. Sometimes you may need to take a loving timeout in meditation from the constant patterns of your mind, and then weave a whole new way of communication that can blanket your relationship with loving-kindness.

Forgiveness as an Antidote to Stress

Studies have shown that meditation improves forgiveness, which in turn can reduce stress. Forgiving yourself and your partner does not mean you will need to stay in your current relationship. Forgiveness is often a pre-requisite for being free to create a new relationship that is unencumbered from the shackles of past pain. You take better care of your SELF without needing walls or filters or burdens of any kind. Then you are free to create the relationship with yourself and others, with attention on constant and loving SELF care.

When you meditate, you can reboot, redo, or renew your relationship in so many loving ways. You can talk about all your issues with cooperation and mutual respect. You can rise above the level of the automatic fight/flight response to a problem and solve it from a higher level of consciousness. You will find creative and intuitive solutions that are made from your best SELF.

From an expanded perspective of SELF-leadership, you can talk about your children, money, work, sex. You can talk about everything you've ever wanted to talk about with ease and grace. Instead of feeling like adversaries, you feel like partners. Peace transcends conflict and joining together can actually feel like fun. You heighten your personal journey towards SELF-realization by accessing higher states of consciousness.

Focusing on your breath and meditation allows you to stay in constant contact with your highest and best SELF.

Ayurveda

Developed thousands of years ago in India, Ayurveda is one of the world's oldest healing systems, incorporating diet, herbal medicine, lifestyle, meditation, yoga, breath work, and other tools for wellness. It is based on the belief that health and wellbeing depend on a delicate balance between the mind, body, and spirit, with its primary focus being the promotion of optimal health, rather than just treating symptoms of disease.

An important goal of Ayurveda is to identify your ideal state of balance, determine where you are out of balance, and offer interventions using diet, herbs, aromatherapy, massage treatments, music, and meditation to reestablish balance. As you take exquisite care of yourself, you will begin to feel more energized, enthusiastic, and relaxed, even in the midst of your relationship transformation. The healthier you feel, the better your decision-making will be. You can create new habits for self care.

Software of the Soul

The habits in your life are caused by a repetition of your prior choices and actions (Karma), which created memories (Sanskara), which fuel your desires (Vasanas)—which then affect your actions (Karma), and the wheel goes on.

You can get off the "hamster wheel of life," and expand your world in an infinite field of possibilities. Try it in your relationship right now. Instead of reacting the same way you always do to something your partner says or does, make a choice to react that is more SELF-led and see what happens. It's the Law of Karma: Give more of what you'd like to receive.

If you want to receive more empathy, compassion, or love, give more of it. If you are longing for more attention, affection, acceptance, or appreciation, see what happens when you put your walls down, change your filters (and thoughts and judgments), and show up in your relationship more calm, compassionate, centered, grateful, and loving.

By changing one action, even a little bit, you can create new memories that lead to new desires, and in that way your relationship transforms. In other words, the next time your partner does something that bothers you, instead of getting tense and sarcastic, or feeling upset and judgmental, take a breath, and choose a different response. You can decide to share your feelings instead of your judgments. You could laugh together. You might concentrate on something you like about your partner instead of all the things you've been resenting. One new response from you could trigger a new way of relating that heretofore seemed impossible.

Expect Miracles, and Watch Them Happen!

As you relate from your heart (instead of your head), you will find that your actions become more nurturing to yourself and others. You will have more compassion for yourself, your partner, and others. You will move organically to the next phase of your relationship in a state of surrender and ease. As you evolve, you move in the direction of SELF, with better self-care, self-realization, and actualization.

The more SELF you experience, the more your life will improve. Your desires and intentions begin to manifest. You feel more energized and alive. You experience a stillness and silence within that helps you stay centered amidst the turmoil of daily life. People around you may notice you feeling lighter and less stressed. You feel a sense of health, vitality, peace and joy. From this expanded state of SELF, your relationship will change organically.

Higher States of Consciousness

The more you meditate, breathe consciously, practice yoga (which is a union of body, mind, and spirit), you will move into a different way of looking at the world. Instead of the dreaming, sleeping, or waking states of consciousness in which most of the world operates, you will transcend the habitual reactivity and begin to have a more cosmic or expansive perspective. Eventually you can see the divinity in everything and everyone, including your partner. You can begin to recognize you are One, each doing the best you know how to do in your human experience.

Tune In to Your Breath: Present-Moment Awareness

You can bring more stillness, silence, and compassion into your relationship with a single breath. Instead of being guided by conditioned response, you are open to a state of creativity. You become more accepting of yourself and your partner as you practice *present- moment awareness.* You can then join with your partner to make decisions about your future. You can make conscious choices (spontaneous right actions) not determined by conditioning or old beliefs, filters, walls, or judgments.

Tune In to Your Body: Yoga

Yoga is a series of postures, and also a state of being in which you are in harmony and balance. You can become more aligned with your body, mind, and spirit and feel more inspired, creative, light, joyful, guided, and happy. Your choices become more nurturing to yourself, your partner, and the world. You become more calm, compassionate and more "in SELF."

As part of a balanced life, yoga is a system of physical fitness that helps you realize your full potential. It allows you to bring those SELF qualities of kindness, compassion and peace as you stay centered in the midst of a turbulent situation.

Yoga postures, or asanas, promote flexibility, strength, and balance through conscious attention to breath, movement, and relaxation. You don't have to twist yourself into a pretzel to practice yoga or judge yourself compared to any ideal. It's an opportunity to be present and accepting with yourself at all times.

Yoga is also a practice that can quiet those incessant thoughts and bring some internal peace. According to the Yoga Sutras or Hindu text "Yoga is a quieting of the fluctuations of the mind field."

There are many forms of yoga, and you can find one that works for you. When you focus on your breathing, you quiet the active chatter in your head. As you learn to relax on the mat, you can become more relaxed off the mat as well. You bring that sense of openness and relaxation into your relationship, and you can possibly begin to see yourself and your partner from a much more expansive and loving perspective.

You begin to feel supported by the Earth and more balanced in your day-to-day life. Like a mountain, you feel grounded, and like a tree, you feel supported and expansive.

Here are a couple of yoga postures that are gentle and relaxing, as well as calming and inspiring. Think about how you can bring your peaceful, balanced SELF into every situation.

Tadasana: Standing Mountain Pose

Stand quietly with your feet hip-distance apart. Close your eyes gently and notice how you sway slightly as your feet naturally balance the weight of your body. Align your ankles over your feet, your knees over your ankles, hips over your knees, shoulders over your hips, and head facing forward. Hands are relaxed towards the ground.

Imagine a golden cord at the top of your head gently lifting up toward the sky as you lengthen and straighten your spine. Relax your shoulders down with a pleasant look on your face. If you want, you can put your tongue at "fire point," which is a point behind your two front teeth where the teeth meet the gum line. By gently resting your tongue at fire point, you automatically relax your jaw and the muscles along your face and throat.

Breathe deep, belly breaths, and imagine that you are a mountain, rooted and supported by the Earth, but free enough to reach up toward the sky. Notice how balanced you feel, no matter what the weather is around you. Allow yourself to feel balanced, peaceful, calm. Just breathe.

After a few moments, gently open your eyes and notice how you feel. Tune in. Take the time to pause and notice and receive the benefits of the pose. Take that peaceful strength with you into the rest of your day.

Vrkasana: Tree Pose

While Tadasana or Standing Mountain Pose helps you attain more stability and inner peace, Vrkasana or Tree Pose enables you to create more balance and expansion.

Start in Tadasana, Standing Mountain Pose. Then open your eyes, focus your gaze at a point across from you at or above eye level. This is your "dristi," or focal point, to help you balance.

Shift your weight to your left leg, and imagine that leg is the trunk of the tree, rooting deeply into the Earth. When you are ready, bring the heel of your right foot to your left ankle, like a kickstand. *(Later you can move your right foot onto your left calf or all the way up to the inside of your left thigh, but never rest it directly on your left knee).*

Please, always be gentle with yourself. In the beginning, you may wobble a bit or lose your balance. Don't give up. Little by little, you will see progress.

Breathe deeply with your hands at your sides. When you are ready, bring your hands in front of your heart, as if in prayer position. Breathe. You have the choice in yoga (as in life) to choose what is most comfortable for you. If you are comfortable and balanced, you can bring your hands above your head and clasp them together in "temple pose." Focus on your "dristi" and breathe.

Imagine that you are a tree: Rooted, grounded, supported by the Earth. Reaching upward to the sky with confidence and serenity. Expanding outward like the limbs, willing to grow in every direction. Allowing the leaves and seeds to fall where they will. Having no agenda. Allowing yourself to "just be." Breathe.

When you are ready, gently release your arms out and down, allowing the expansion to happen naturally. Release your right foot back onto the floor. And then repeat on the other side.

Imagine the tone of your conversations if you and your partner took a moment to ground, center, come to inner balance and then talk about your feelings, wants and needs. Can you see how your relationship could change and improve?

Yoga helps you get to SELF and stay in SELF, and so does meditation and taking a single conscious breath. Maintaining a healthy balance in your lifestyle also reduces stress and promotes wellness.

Aside from the *asanas* or yoga poses, the practice of yoga allows you to bring a more SELF-led, peaceful energy to all of your actions and behaviors. Practicing the Seven Spiritual Laws can also improve all your relationships.

The Seven Spiritual Laws and Your Relationship

Deepak Chopra wrote the *Seven Spiritual Laws of Success* to help you fulfill your deepest desires with ease and grace. Deepak and David Simon expanded those practices in *The Seven Spiritual Laws of Yoga*. Each day of the week is dedicated to one of the spiritual laws. If you take a few moments each day to quiet your mind or meditate on each one, you can apply these laws to your relationship. You won't have to struggle to make changes; they will unfold naturally with more kindness and compassion.

If you want to apply these principles to your relationship, you will have a framework for your own SELF-care and the loving consideration that you can offer your partner.

The Seven Laws are:
- The Law of Pure Potentiality
- The Law of Giving and Receiving
- The Law of Karma or Cause and Effect
- The Law of Least Effort
- The Law of Intention and Desire
- The Law of Detachment
- The Law of Dharma or Purpose in Life

166

The Law of Pure Potentiality

"When we realize that our true SELF is one of pure potentiality, we align with the power that manifests everything in nature," wrote Deepak Chopra. You are not limited by your ego's beliefs and constraints, but are connected to your spiritual essence.

To experience and understand this Law of Pure Potentiality, here are some of the things you can do. You can take time each day to be silent, to "just BE." Cultivate silence and commune with nature. Instead of arguing when your partner does something to bother you, you could go for a walk and breathe. Then come back and talk about the issue with clarity and empathy.

As you practice non-judgment of yourself and your partner, you will be open to beginning a whole new relationship. Instead of defining yourself in terms of a wife, husband, parent, you'll see yourself as the *infinite being* that you are, and make new choices from your expanded awareness.

The Law of Giving and Receiving

If you give what you are seeking—more empathy, understanding, compassion, love—it will return to you. You can begin to circulate joy; to give the gift of your presence, your attention, affection, appreciation, and acceptance. And when you do so, you will be open to receiving and staying grateful for the new experiences that will come your way. Instead of noticing what you spouse is not doing, do more of it yourself. For instance, if you complain that he leaves the house or comes home without kissing you hello or goodbye, you can be the one to reach out with a hug and a kiss each time. Try it with an open heart and see what happens.

The Law of Karma or Cause and Effect

When you choose actions that consider another's feelings and needs, you will have a better chance of creating a relationship in which your feelings and needs are also valued. Witness the choices you've made and the new ones you will be making. As you bring awareness into your relationship, you will focus on the consequences of your behavior and reactions. You can then seek those outcomes that are more fulfilling and connecting. Tune in to your heart for guidance, and see how your body feels as you consider your choices. You can then make spontaneously correct choices for yourself and for all concerned. You will know when you are choosing actions from SELF, because you will feel good when you make them.

The Law of Least Effort

Practice acceptance of everything the way it is right now. No matter what you wish for your future, totally accept your present circumstances.

Next, take responsibility, without blame of yourself or anyone else, and know that you can transform this moment into an experience of personal and spiritual growth. Your awareness and acceptance can be present without any need to defend your position. You don't need to convince or persuade others, and you can stay open to other points of view beside your own. As you relax into a new way of relating, you will find that you can resolve long-standing issues with more ease and grace. Your Parts may want to fight, but your SELF wants to create harmony and peace.

The Law of Intention and Desire:

Make a list of all that you want and need in your relationship. Focus on all that you desire, instead of what doesn't serve you. Even if you don't get what's on your list, you will know that there is a bigger, cosmic plan for your life, and you can remind yourself to stay present. As you accept the present as it is, you can put your *attention* on your *intention* for a better relationship, and then watch that future ideal unfold.

The Law of Detachment

You can let go of your attachment to any specific outcome. If you know you want more love in your life, you may be able to surrender to what is. You have the opportunity to allow your partner the right to be who she is, and not try to mold her into who you think you need her to be. You can appreciate the good aspects of your partner and not require him to change to fit your ideas of how you think he *should be.* Instead of the chaos and strife you might have been experiencing, you will open yourself to uncertainty, out of which solutions will spontaneously emerge. You don't need to know what the future holds as you stay grateful for blessings in the present. As you embrace the future with a sense of wonder, you can experience more fun, light, and laughter, even in the moment at hand. Anything is possible when you come from your highest SELF, without an agenda, judgment, or blame.

The Law of Dharma or Purpose in Life:

You have many unique gifts and talents that you can offer to yourself and in service to others. You can lovingly nurture your SELF, knowing that you are having a painful human experience—in the form of a relationship challenge—and can respond to the experience from a more expanded and spiritual perspective. You can create abundance in your life by remembering your unique talents and sharing them with love. Whatever happens with you and your partner, you will be on your path of fulfillment, which you can bring to your current and future relationships. As you practice exquisite SELF-care, utilizing your unique gifts and talents, you will find more fulfillment in the present. From a more confident and contented perspective, you will be better prepared to make decisions for your future.

Chapter 8
Let Go of Limiting Beliefs

*"The lessons we are to discover in this lifetime are within us
and doing the work to unburden our parts are the lessons.
Our relationships become the petri dish for this personal growth.
Put two people together, mix their parts,
and see how each can change and expand."*
—Richard Schwartz, Ph.D.
Founder, Internal Family Systems Therapy

To create a new relationship, you need to take exquisite care of your SELF. Some of the ways you practice:

- Breathe consciously and deeply.

- Meditate

- Eat well and exercise regularly.

- Practice Ayurveda, or a healthy balanced lifestyle.

- Stay grateful for your blessings.

- Stay present (avoid complaining about the past or worrying about the future).

- Be willing to experience more awareness, acceptance, and forgiveness—of both yourself and your partner.

- Start creating the next chapter of your life from your highest and best SELF.

- Practice the Seven Spiritual Laws

173

One other important way to begin a new relationship is to **heal your pain from the past**. You do that by understanding your Parts—all the feelings you exile, ways you've managed, and how your extreme behavior has led to some negative reactions. You have been conditioned by your prior experiences, thoughts and beliefs, and you have managed your life in ways that you hoped would keep you safe. The way you relate to your partner has probably been more from your Parts than from your SELF.

When you don't take care of your SELF, you lose the ability to be caring for others. When you are not "in SELF," you're often being led by a Part and believing the thoughts you think. You live with judgments and blame, react in fight,/flight/freeze mode rather than with *spontaneously correct responses*, and you feel more stress.

My client Susan took the time she needed to do her own healing work first. Then she was able to transform her relationship with her husband. She learned to unburden her Inner Child, let go of limiting beliefs, and relate from her highest and best SELF. As she continued to practice all she was learning, she realized she was living *"with mindfulness."*

Susan had come to see me alone for several visits. She never brought her husband in for marriage counseling, but often mentioned their relationship as a source of pain or stress for her. Mark would sometimes get angry quickly, and it always bothered her. She didn't think that he considered her feelings, and he seemed always to need everything in perfect order or else he would explode. The slightest thing could set him off: if he looked for butter in the refrigerator and didn't find it immediately, she could hear him frustrated and angry, and she would feel upset with him.

Susan worked with me individually and had taken the time to reflect on her Family of Origin and explore how her mother's undiagnosed bipolar disorder had given Susan many burdens when she was growing up. Her mother would be calm one minute and then turn on her daughter in angry and aggressive ways. Those early childhood experiences affected Susan in her reactions in her present relationship with her husband.

For many years in her marriage, she...

- Tried to be "perfect
- Had trouble being criticized
- "Magically believed" that her husband would be the one to save her and never make her feel bad

Susan experienced her husband's outbursts of anger as abusive, and she would either get angry back with yelling or sarcasm or become withholding and not speak to him or be intimate with him for several days.

She had learned to put up a *wall* to protect herself from her husband's outbursts, which reminded her of her mother's rants when Susan was young. At first, Susan did not want to put down her wall because she said Mark could then get into my space. Over time, Susan was willing to get to know her wall and learn how to relate to Mark from her higher SELF, by doing the following exercise to find her Part.

Find Your Part:

Where Do You Feel or Sense That Part in Your Body?

When you start to feel sad or scared or angry, where in your body do you feel that sensation? Where in your body do you feel tense, tight, anxious? What does that energy want you to know?

> Susan told me she would feel her stomach "tie up in knots" and pressure in her head like she wanted to scream. Instead of speaking for her sad and hurt Exiled Parts, she would often Manage by getting angry and yelling back at Mark. When she decided to

stifle her anger, but was still seething inside with unspoken feelings, she would resort to Extreme behavior and go to the kitchen to eat compulsively as a way to numb and detach.

Put that Part Outside of Your Body and Describe It.

If you could take that energy of your Part and put it outside your body or even imagine it in its own glass room, what would it look like? How would you describe it? Does it have a shape, a color, a texture, a density? Does it look or sound like anyone you know? Sometimes your own Inner Critic looks just like one of your parents who was critical of you as a child. You have then taken on that internal dialogue of criticism to help you "shape up" and "do better." Does that Part look like you at a different time or like you do now? What is this Part or energy saying? What is its message to you? What does it keep repeating? Just listen. As you give your part your compassionate awareness, it will begin to share with you its intention to keep you safe.

Susan's "Wall" looked like a "blob" that kept her insulated and safe. She pictured herself walking around her house inside the protective bubble of this "blob," safely insulated by the Wall she had built to keep Mark out.

How Do You Feel Towards that Part?

When you are "in SELF," you will either be *compassionate* to that Part for all the work it has done in the past, or you will be *curious* about its motives and intentions. If you are not "in SELF," ask the Parts of you that are activated (fear, judgment, anger) to relax back a bit and let you be with this Part from your highest

> At first Susan didn't like the Wall and "wanted it to go away." On the other hand, she was afraid for it to go away because she knew it was protecting her.

Getting to Know Your Part

Tell your Part: *"I would like to understand you better. Is that OK?"* All of your Parts are looking for your calm, witnessing presence. When you show up without judgment of your Parts, they will explain more of why they have the roles they do.

Listen for messages coming from your Part. Often Parts are relieved to have you finally find them. Others are more skeptical of your attention and are initially reluctant to talk.

> The "Wall" was willing to answer Susan's questions, but it was skeptical that any positive change would occur. It was so used to being in charge of keeping her safe that it was reluctant to give up its role. Until her Part trusted that it was safe to transform, it would continue to do its job.

Ask Your Part, "What is Your Job?"

Listen for the answer. Almost all of your Parts, when asked with compassion, will answer that they are just trying to protect you.

> Like all Parts, Susan's "blob" was quick to acknowledge its desire to help her stay safe. As long as she was "walled" to her husband, he couldn't hurt her.

Ask Your Part: "What are You Afraid Will Happen to Me If You Don't Do That Job?"

Keep listening and asking, "and what would you be afraid of then?" until you get to the root intention of the Part, which is *always to protect you* from being hurt, feeling unloved, being abandoned, being alone. **A Manager or Extreme Part is always working to protect those Exiled Parts that felt sad, hurt, scared.**

As a child, you suffered pain and sadness and the hurt felt like a kick in the gut. The energy from that trauma is still stored somewhere in your body. Rather than feel the feelings, you may have "gone into your head" to try to figure out a way to cope with the feelings. You could decide to become strong, hardworking, codependent, angry, stoic, intellectual, humorous. You could maintain some form of facade, or

179

"pseudo-self," where you looked like you were "in SELF", but you were really feeling sad, scared, hurt, or angry underneath the mask.

When you "went into your head" to defend yourself from your exiled feelings (of sadness, fear, anger), your ego projected an image of calm and confidence that was not truly mirroring your internal landscape. **Underneath the mask, those Inner Child feelings went unattended. These Managers and Extreme Parts became the Protectors of the feelings of this Inner Child.**

> Susan's Protective Part (her internal wall around her heart that resembled a "blob") was convinced that if it didn't do *its job*, that Susan would be scared and vulnerable like she was when her mother used to yell at her for no reason.

Thank Your Part

As you recognize all the efforts made on behalf of the Inner Child, and all the burdens carried by this Part, you can thank it for its *intention* to be of help. You will probably see all the ways this Part has served you in the past. You may even see scenes from your past—like frames in a movie—times that this Part has come to your defense.

Susan realized that her "blob" had been protecting her since she was a child. She had used it to stop being *enraged* at Mark since it helped *keep the peace*, and she thanked it for her attention to be protective.

However, she was still angry inside, so the Wall helped her seem less angry, but her sarcasm felt very passive/aggressive to her husband. Susan was beginning to see how her well-meaning Protective Part was affecting her husband and family in unintended negative ways.

Negotiate a Better Job for the Part

You can ask your Part the following question: *"If you could trust ME, coming from SELF, to take care of my Inner Child and to allow him/her to heal and grow safely, would you be willing to relax a bit or to find another job that would be more healing?"*

Allow for healthy skepticism, as this Part has been on autopilot for years and is reluctant to let go of its job because it doesn't know it can trust YOU yet. Ask it to be willing to allow you to show it how you can help your Inner Child unburden the pain from the past, and then show this Part how you will do that.

Let your Part know you will continue to show up to care for your Inner Child from this point forward.

As Susan was able to show her Walled Part true gratitude for its *intention* to be helpful, the Part felt seen, appreciated, and accepted. It was then free to transform and become more willing to relax its endeavors or to find a better job to be more helpful to Susan.

SELF Leadership: Watch the Part Transform

You can learn how to witness compassionately and appreciate and validate sincerely the *intentions* of your Parts to protect you. Even though the Parts have created situations that have caused problems in the past, with your SELF presence, your Parts and your partner's Parts can peacefully and lovingly transform. With your compassionate attention and acceptance, you will probably notice this Part calming down, and perhaps even changing shape.

Once you give your Protective Parts appreciation for trying to keep you safe, many of your harshest Inner Judges can become your best cheerleaders. Your critics become your coaches. The more you show up "in SELF" with respect and love for your Parts, the more they can trust YOU in ways that bring harmony and inner peace to your whole *internal family system*.

Try it yourself today. Just notice the walls you have built around your heart, or the filters through which you have been judging your partner. Take a deep breath (or many deep conscious breaths throughout your day), and become aware of how you can change the ways you relate to yourself and your partner. When all your Parts trust your SELF-leadership, they can heal, transform, and unburden.

Chapter 9
Unburdening Your Inner Child

*"Compassion is one of the highest states of consciousness
that you can use to assist you in times of enormous pain."*
—Debbie Ford, Author

As you practice Compassionate Communication, you will more often be "in SELF." You will become more adept at noticing when you are putting up a wall or judging your partner through some outdated filter of criticism or blame. You can then either stop yourself from your old behaviors, apologize for them, or even just be aware at noticing what you are doing. The witness to your actions is your SELF.

However, in many cases, it is very difficult to "unblend" from your Protective Parts because they believe you will become vulnerable again, as you were in the past. Your Protectors want to keep you safe.

Helping these Protective Parts—your Wall, your Filters—let go of their limiting beliefs was explained in the preceding chapter, and in this chapter, you learn how you can, "in SELF," take care of your own Exiled Parts that your Managers were trying to keep safe. You do this by unburdening the pain from your past, and learning how to care for and love your Inner Child.

Your partner probably does or says things that trigger you. It could be how he or she says something or does (or not does) something, and your response might be more extreme than their behavior warrants in that moment. It's almost like they pushed some imaginary button on your chest, and that button leads to a "trailhead" taking you to a past pain or fear that has not been processed or released until now.

For example, when my ex-husband was displeased or angry, I reacted like that same little girl who was so afraid of my beloved father's bipolar episodes. I would usually try to manage my fear and sadness (and even my anger at having my boundaries violated) by codependent behavior of placating, pleasing, or acting nice.

It took a long time to finally help my Managers let go of many beliefs—that anger wasn't safe, that I had to be the "good girl," that I couldn't set a boundary—to make room for me to find and love my Inner Child and connect to my highest SELF as I keep her safe.

I told her that anger was an honest reaction to having her boundaries violated and that she deserved to set boundaries around how someone (anyone) would speak to her: no yelling, no name calling, no profanity. I told her that she deserves to feel loved and safe, and if she doesn't, she can leave. I reminded her of how important it is always to speak her truth, no matter what anyone else chooses to say or do in response. Little by little, she has come to trust me and believe me, and to feel safe in the world.

It's important that you see the child inside of you as well, and learn how to care for him or her. As Dick Schwartz said about his own Part, *"In my work with my own parts, I discovered that the rage I'd struggled to control when growing up was more than a dangerous bundle of explosive anger: I realized it was protecting a deeply insecure young boy inside me, who was stuck in scenes when it felt as if my very survival was being threatened by my father's expressions of contempt for me. As I got to know it, I came to see this part not as a threat, but as a noble defender — the part of me that struggled with my inner critic and was ready to come to my aid in any situation in which I felt endangered by being criticized.*

Once I could recognize that and embrace this part of myself, I could release the rage I'd carried all through my life."

The process of unburdening will bring up a lot of feelings that have been stored or exiled for a long time. It is best to do this with someone who can be with you to hold the space, hold your hand, or offer you support. Whether you decide to pursue a new relationship with your spouse or create a compassionate divorce, unburdening pain from your past will allow you to create a future that is filled with more joy and happiness in your life.

SECTION FOUR
Make Decisions from Your Highest SELF

Chapter 10
Your Compassionate Relationship

"Our compassion and acts of selflessness
take us to the deeper truths."
—Amma, Mata Amritanandamayi, Spiritual Leader

After engaging in the process of Compassionate Mediation, you and your partner may decide that you both want to give 100 percent effort to creating something new and better together. You can take all that you learned from your discussions to add to your current connection. You now have a better idea of each of your views on finances, parenting, socializing, shared responsibilities and all other issues important to each of you. Now that you've shared empathy, needs and desires, it's time to focus on co-creating a more intimate and loving connection that will meet both of your needs from this time on. You don't have to fit together perfectly, but now know how to accommodate each other in ways that co-create a new and better union.

As Arielle Ford says in her book, *Wabi Sabi Love,* "*Wabi Sabi Love is the art and practice of loving the imperfections in ourselves and in our partners. It is not mere acceptance or denial of the things that may annoy us or even drive us crazy but rather a deep and profound appreciation for the uniqueness of each other.*"

In order to create a new and better relationship, you will practice forgiveness for whatever hurt you in the past. As Judge Michele Lowrance says in her book *The Good Karma Divorce,* "*The aspiration toward forgiveness does not require forgetting the past or preclude learning from it; it gives you control and power over how you let the past define who you are in the present and in the future.*"

As you think about your future together, share your thoughts and feelings about what is important to you. What would a wonderful partnership feel like to you? How would you describe it? What words would you use? Think of two or three or more words that set the intention for the kind of relationship you'd like to have. Now share that list with your partner. Ask him or her what words they would use to describe their idea of a loving and intimate relationship. Their list may be more similar to yours than you think.

You could make another separate list of what you know *you don't want* in a relationship and compare that with your partner's. Again, you both may want to end the anger, resentment, walls, and judgments. Now is the time to make that happen.

Take a breath for a moment and consider what gets in the way of actually having that loving relationship you are seeking. You can learn how to create more of what you want by coming from SELF, and how to let go of whatever is in the way by healing your Parts.

Descartes wrote: *"I think, therefore I am."* But you are so much more than just your mind, and sometimes it's what you *think* that causes the problems. Caroline Myss says, *"The soul always knows what to do to heal itself. The challenge is to silence the mind."*

Your thoughts, beliefs, and judgments have affected the ways you both *habitually react*ed in the past. Your minds kept you stuck in old patterns. You are learning how to relate from your hearts, where you're open to insight, wisdom, and ultimately infinite possibilities.

If you are willing to look at your belief system and edit and revise some of your thoughts and judgments, there is a chance for a new and improved relationship to be created. As author Wayne Dyer said, *"When we change the way we look at something, what we look at changes."* You can change your relationship by changing the way you look at it—starting now. Instead of reacting from your Parts, you relate from your highest and best SELF. If you are willing to put down your walls and stop looking through the filter of your judgments, you create a new beginning. You can give up the old habits and patterns and view yourself and your partner with more love and compassion. This will change your perspective and your relationship. If you treat your partner with compassion and kindness instead of judgment or blame, you will be pleasantly surprised at their reaction.

The decision to let your walls down takes courage. It takes SELF-leadership and patience. As Sam Keen has said, *"We come to love not by finding a perfect person, but by learning to see an imperfect person perfectly."* It helps if you always remember you are both doing the best you know how to do based on your level of awareness in this present moment.

You can learn the *currency* of your partners need for love. Does she like to be touched, hear words of endearment, need more attention, affection, appreciation, acceptance? When you give him what he wants and needs, rather than what you wish he would give you, he often learns how to reciprocate in your preferred *language of love*. Compassionate Communication helps you navigate these discussions so that you both feel heard, seen, respected, and loved.

When you feel more loved, you feel more loving, and guess what—the passion returns!

Create Passion by Sharing Compassion and Partnership

When there's **peace**, it's safe to put your walls down. You remove the filters through which you saw your partner. You no longer see them with blame or judgment or fear, and you realize there are no triggers to threaten your security with each other.

When there's **partnership.** you feel like a team and fun begins to return to your connection. When you're safely connected and feeling respected and enjoying each other, the **passion** you initially experienced begins to reappear. It often *intensifies*—because of the deeper level of your connection. You remember what you used to enjoy together and begin doing more of it again.

There's one thing I didn't mention earlier. I don't put it on my business card, but for a short time I was interning with a sex therapist and helping people revive their sex lives. I quickly realized that sexual intimacy is not about technique. Better intimacy on all levels comes from forgiveness, compassion, and peace. The more you learn how to be understanding, empathetic, and affectionate, the more passion there will be.

Make plans together for new experiences that are interesting, exciting, enjoyable. You can take turns arranging date nights, choosing the activities and calling a sitter if you have children. Some of my clients have little activity jars where they just think of something to do, put it in the jar, and take out an idea from time to time so that there's no pressure to pick a plan and they can mutually create more fun.

Help your partner feel like a priority to you. Focus on making him or her happy—as you ask for and receive what you want and need. Create new habits of touch, connection, laughter, and fun. You will feel appreciated, accepted, admired, adored, and then you reciprocate in kind. Or first offer that appreciation, acceptance, admiration, and loving attention yourself, and see what happens.

Passion can permeate your whole relationship in and out of the bedroom because intimacy is not just intercourse, it's holding hands, it's cuddling, it's hugging, it's that kiss hello and goodbye. You begin to offer love in the currency of your partner, not giving to meet your needs but to meet theirs. They do the same for you.

In her new book, *Turn Your Mate into Your Soulmate,* Arielle Ford reminds us of the meaning of love. *"Love is both a choice and a behavior...Love is a connection. Love is a feeling...Love is about being willing to forgive. Love is God. Love is who we are. Love is why we are here. To put it simply, love is all there is."*

SARK sees herself as *"a full cup of love sharing her overflow with the world."* Isn't that wonderful?

Fill your cup first. Fill your life with passion, vibrancy and joy. It can be done. You can do it. All it takes is love, starting with loving yourself. Then let your overflow of love bring peace, partnership, and passion to your relationship, to your family, and to the world.

How to Begin (again):

- Take the Relationship Survey at the beginning of this book for a second time.

- Ask your partner to read this book and take the Survey.

- Compare your lists of what you want in a relationship and what you don't want.

- Make decisions together that will give you both more of what you want and need.

- Practice the Miracle of Empathy as you listen, understand, and care.

- Share your realizations about your Families of Origin and how they have affected you and your relationship in the past.

- Plan ways to have healthier connections in the future.

- If you need support, get help to let go of old beliefs, burdens and behaviors.

- Put down your *walls*.

- Relate from your highest and best SELF.

- Change your *filters*.

- Let go of any judgments about your partner or yourself.

- Find ways to remind your partner of how much you love him/her.

- Go back to the legal and financial information and become mutually informed and empowered as you plan for your future.

- Identify how you experience passion in your life.

- Share it with your partner and listen to what they say in response to what they want.

- Discover and share your currency for feeling loved. Do you like touch? Do you like time together? Do you like words or acts of generosity? Do you like a good meal? Do you like sharing experiences—travel, sports, classes, outdoor activities, workshops, entertainment?

- Remember the importance of laughter and fun, and find ways to create them.

- Repeat often: "Thank you," "I'm sorry," and "I love you."

- Share with your partner the Hawaiian Ho'oponopono process which consists of the phrases *"I love you, please forgive me, I am sorry, thank you."*

- Know that you can always "start over" from your highest and best SELF.

- Start over with your heart open and available.

- Allow yourself to receive and appreciate all the blessings you already share and the ones you will co-create in the future.

- Stay present, hopeful, and grateful.

Chapter 11
Your *Compassion*ate SELF-Led Divorce®

"With all of the darkness you may be walking through,
it's good to remember that where there is no light,
you have the choice to become it."
—Katherine Woodward, Author

You may find that even as you become the best version of your SELF—and take that energy and loving presence into your current relationship—you may decide that it is time to leave. If so, you can begin the process of a SELF-Led Divorce.

For some couples, the process of Compassionate Mediation is a prelude to a separation. You can build on the conversations that you have begun, and then make decisions for the future for yourselves and your children.

A Compassionate SELF- Led Divorce is a new, wiser paradigm for peacefully and respectfully restructuring your family: No more fighting, arguing, withdrawing, and feeling stuck.

You will do yourself and your children a favor by forgiving and moving on, no matter what choices your spouse makes. You and your partner have done the best you knew how to do and have shared many memories, experiences, and relationships. You have learned from the good and the challenging, and you are now ready to live the next chapter of your life with more ease and grace. As you make decisions from your best SELF, your future, and the future of your re-structured family, will be filled with more love, compassion, and grace.

A SELF-Led Divorce creates safety for you, your spouse, and especially your children, who will no longer suffer from the shrapnel of their parents' extreme and warring Parts.

The Compassionate SELF-Led Divorce takes you through each step of the process for peacefully and respectfully ending a marriage, providing all. the information, guidance, and support you need along the way. You will save time, money, and emotional turmoil. The effort it takes to get ready, to get to your best SELF, will shorten what is often a thorny journey and save you years of pain—before, during, and after the divorce.

How to Add Compassion to Your SELF-Led Divorce®

First, make sure you do all the exercises in this book, answering all the questions, and learning how to practice all the tools offered. It's easier if you and your partner both want to pursue a divorce. Whatever your current feelings, you can:

- Practice the Miracle of Empathy so that you can both share your feelings safely.

- Make a list of all that you want and need, and share it calmly with your partner, as you listen empathetically to their wants and needs.

- Review all of the legal and financial information in Section Two to make sure that you are both fully informed and empowered.

- Begin to discuss possible scenarios with an open heart and an open mind:
    - Where would you each live?
    - What would you do about sharing parenting?
    - What are possible ways to divide the assets?
    - Is maintenance a possibility and if so, how would you determine how much and for how long?

- Continue to practice Compassionate Communication.

- Take all the time you need.

- Continue to do your own work to heal and forgive and move on.

Results you can expect from a SELF-Led Divorce

- You feel more calm, clear, compassionate, connected, courageous, confident, balanced, centered, peaceful, and grateful—in other words, more SELF-led.

- Your children are forever grateful for all that you do to avoid acrimony.

- Your health improves because your stress is less.

- You're more focused and productive at work.

- You sleep better, longer, more soundly.

- You will co-create a future with your former spouse that will be reflective of the bonds and friendship you once shared.

Even with the best divorce you can have, there are still feelings that must be experienced and processed. Take all the time you need to allow for emotional, psychological, financial, legal, and spiritual healing to occur. As Louise Hay, author and founder of Hay House says, *"I forgive you for not being the way I wanted you to be. I forgive you and I set you free."*

The Death of Your Marriage

Divorce is a death—the death of a marriage, the death of a dream—which must be grieved and mourned just like any other demise. Too often people who have never experienced it themselves have no true concept of the enormity of the loss and pain and sadness that accompanies a divorce.

Not only do you lose your spouse, but the dream, the security, the finances, the families, the friends, and sometimes the children on half the holidays for the rest of your lives. Sometimes divorce feels like you are going to your own funeral and being surprised at who doesn't show up.

And just as people react to a death of a person, you have similar reactions to the death of your marriage. Elizabeth Kubler-Ross described those emotions as denial, anger, bargaining, depression, and acceptance. That translates into:

Denial: *"This isn't happening to me."*

Anger: *"Damn it, this is happening to me!"*

Bargaining: *"If I am very good or do this or don't do that, this won't happen to me."*

Depression: *"I'm so sad and depressed that this is happening to me!"*

Acceptance: *"I am grateful for what I learned because this happened to me."*

Every divorce causes distress. Whether there were drugs or alcohol, abuse, infidelity, or the standard "irreconcilable differences," the pain is intense because it wasn't supposed to happen at all.

But it has, so what do you do now? A Compassionate SELF-Led Divorce offers new possibilities. You can balance the grieving with the growing, the hurting with the healing, and the losing with the loving—starting with loving yourself.

Anyone experiencing or ever touched by divorce has suffered a loss that can be unexpected and devastating. You may be losing your marriage, but you now have the opportunity to find yourself, possibly for the first time in your life. Grieving the losses and feeling your feelings are necessary parts of the process of divorce. But also hold onto the reality that from this point on, your life may offer miracles you may never have dared to dream.

Grieving the Loss

Everyone has suffered losses of different kinds. Whenever there's a loss, there's grieving that *must* be done in order to move on and heal. You might feel that it's easier to deny the pain and try to *forget it, or live with it, or not make waves.* These approaches never work. The pain stays and reveals itself in unexpected ways: depression, shame, guilt, intense need, compulsions, food addictions, drinking, and drugs.

Perhaps you've never been taught how to express emotions in a healthy way. You may have learned to be ashamed of your needs, to recoil from your anger, to silence your sadness, or ignore your fear. Your role models may have shown you how *not* to be, and you're afraid that if you ever express your emotions, you'll do it inappropriately, or that you might hurt others as they've hurt you.

You may believe that your anger will come out as rage, or your needs will be so overwhelming that others will abandon you. You fear that by stating your feelings you may hurt someone else's feelings. You may not know how to be angry. Perhaps you intellectualize everything and stay in your head as a way of distancing yourself from emotions.

The Only Way Beyond Is Through

You can't ignore your anger, sadness, pain, and fear. The only way to get beyond these feelings is to go *through* them. You can't stuff them down forever. You can't forget about them or make them go away by ignoring them. You must allow yourself the right—and the time and opportunity—to express them.

You may need to get some professional help as you practice recognizing and acknowledging your feelings. You can begin by accepting your feelings and then learn how to express them to others in healthy ways. It's a process, to be sure, an evolution. You have to be open to the process and willing to express yourself, to let go, and grow.

Changing Your Paradigm

Your paradigm is your view of the world and place in it. Divorce transforms the fabric of your life, demanding growth and change.

While growth is ultimately empowering and liberating, change can feel very frightening. It forces you to confront the unknown. You give up your old ways of thinking and feeling and behaving, and begin to learn new ways. But the time in the middle part of the journey feels like the rug has been pulled out from under you, like you're falling into a deep abyss, or like that scary ride on a roller coaster.

But once you're off that roller coaster, you can step out as a more authentic person, with a new set of dreams, roles, and relationships. Divorce can bring your own rebirth, rejuvenation, and renewal. Someday, you're likely to feel grateful to your ex-spouse for giving you the opportunity to grow into who you were meant to be. You just had to go through the fire to get to the other side.

Your outdated paradigm was shaped by what you were taught by others, and you internalized their ideas. You can learn to identify those old tapes that have skewed your perceptions, and you can learn effective, simple techniques to rewrite these internal messages.

As you change, you can transform Parts of yourself and edit out the useless, no longer necessary compulsions. You learn what you need and want and ways to achieve them. You learn what you will and won't tolerate. You learn how to say "no"—without guilt. You stop waiting for someone to take care of you and now take care of yourself. And as you become healthier, you attract healthier people into your life.

Divorce is a time when you need to begin to look inside yourself to find out what *you* want and need, and how to give it to yourself. So, take your time and tune inside to your own inner voice, your own true SELF.

Moving Forward

Life offers us an array of opportunities—and challenges. The major challenge is seeing the opportunities when you are in pain. Perhaps you think *if only* your expectations are fulfilled, then you can be happy. You look for something external to yourself to fill a (perceived) void within.

Once you realize, finally and fully, without any doubts at all, that you are complete as you are, a totally whole individual, an incredible sense of peace descends. There is no need to strive, to seek, to search outside of yourself for happiness. No obligation to merge in order to feel complete. No necessity to find in another what you felt missing in yourself.

There is a freedom from struggle. A letting-go of effort. It's relaxing, joyous, energizing. It's being home wherever you are, whenever your heart is open. It is safety.

It is your true SELF.

Many of us have lost ourselves in relationships. Many of us forfeited our truths when we were children. We abandoned and exiled our true feelings by managing them with behaviors we thought would be better accepted by our parents, siblings, teachers, peers. We learned how to please, placate, get by, function, manage.

We perceived ourselves as lacking in some way, and we were attracted to others who seemed to complete us, fill in the blanks, provide what we were seeking. Often those traits that brought us to our partners were the ones that began to bother us the most. For example, a shy man is attracted to a talkative lady, but later he complains that she is never quiet. A woman falls for a man who is strong and assertive and many years hence decides he's too paternalistic and controlling.

Once we know that we are complete, we lose the desperation of the search. People may come and go in our lives, but we don't tie to any one of them the ability to make us or break us. We can be happy to share our time, our bodies, our lives with someone else, but we can do it as equals, without expectations or judgments.

We can learn how to speak our truth—without fear. We can discern when our needs are being met, or our boundaries violated. We can choose to stay in a relationship, or we can choose to go. And if someone chooses to leave us first, we can know that we are just fine, time will heal our pride, and we can go on to find a relationship that is meant to go the distance— however long that distance is meant to be.

Perhaps the "happily ever after" needs to be edited to "happily each day." Rather than seek the prince on the horse or the damsel in need, we can drop the fantasy and be receptive to reality. We can look within ourselves to find the communication, companionship, and connection we are seeking.

Let your quest become an internal one. Let your pursuit focus on self-awareness, self-care, and self-love. Then you can nurture your heart, your light, your ability to feel joy, and attract into your life healthy people who are doing the same.

The Divine Plan for Your Life

I have come to believe that there is a divine plan for our lives, and we do not always understand it as we stumble along our paths. There are things that we are meant to learn, and the Universe will give us subtle nudges, stronger hints, overt messages and finally some cataclysmic blows to get our attention to make the changes toward authenticity and self empowerment.

Divorce is one of those "dark nights of the soul," which can either leave you a victim or a more authentic human being, capable of connecting with your Higher Power and true SELF. In Compassionate Mediation, you receive empathy, support and guidance whether you are contemplating a divorce, in the midst of one, or recently divorced, separated or ending a relationship.

The Birth of Your SELF

Divorce also can be a time of rejuvenation and renewal. Divorce can also be a birth—as you learn how to give life to your True SELF, one that had been hidden, repressed, sublimated or denied for decades.

The Universe has given you an unexpected blow. You can either disintegrate from the weight of it, or use it as opportunity to build a different and often better life for yourself. You can choose to lie down and feel lost, or you can find another path. You have the ability to be reincarnated on this Earth, in this lifetime. You can keep the virtues and traits you like, and reinvent the rest.

Often divorce is when you may meet your spiritual nature for the first time. And if you are already aware of the spiritual connection, you have an opportunity to expand it and contribute what you can to others. You find power you didn't know you had and then have the chance to be reborn into a more authentic, compassionate, centered, peaceful, and independent being.

Helping Your Children

The decision to divorce is life-changing for all of you—you, your spouse, and your family—and telling your children is often one of the hardest moments in the process.

There are many things you can do to guide and support them at this time, depending on their ages and maturity level.

The best gift you can give your children is to *minimize conflict* **between you and your spouse.**

When it's time to talk to your children, tell them only what they need to know. They will ask questions about everything — why are you getting divorced, what will happen to them, where will you live, who's "fault" is it — but you can answer only what is relevant for their peace of mind.

There are age-appropriate conversations. You wouldn't discuss your decision the same way with young children as you might with teenagers. Whatever words you use, you can let them know that you and your spouse are having problems, but you're working on these *together*. If you and your spouse decide to separate or divorce, then you should both tell the children *together*. If that is not possible, because you can't schedule a time that works for you both, or because a child has asked one of you alone, then plan what you will each say to the children if asked.

As you plan to tell them together, take the time to get to (and speak from) SELF. When you are "in SELF," you'll be sharing in a way that fosters safety and hope for your children — and both of you. In my experience, most parents feel tremendous anxiety about having this discussion, but are relieved once they've had it.

The following suggestions have helped many people create sensitive dialogue that considers the feelings and needs of everyone concerned. The main points include the following:

- Let your children know that you both love them and that you each will be there for them.

- Make sure they understand that the separation or divorce is *not* their fault.

- Let them know it's okay if they feel sad or angry or scared, and that you'll be there to help them with their feelings.

- Assure them that you'll be taking care of yourself and your own feelings, too, and that they don't have to take care of *you.*

- Don't use your children as your confidantes, and don't turn to them for emotional support.

Let's hope you can pledge to your children that they'll now have two homes where they can feel loved and be comfortable and safe. Then you and your spouse can work together to make that promise a reality.

How to Talk with Your Children

Choose a time to tell the children when you and your spouse can be together. (If you have children of various ages, you may tell them at different times as your conversations with your teenager might be different than the one you'd have with your younger child.) Whether you tell all the children at the same time, you and your spouse should try to talk to them together, if possible. Most important of all, talk to your children from SELF, as you clearly and courageously engage in this very challenging conversation.

I am offering the following "script" for you to use when you're ready. Sometimes, you first tell your children that you are planning to separate. This can be less painful than the "divorce discussion," but often a "separation" is just a euphemism for divorce. Use the term "separation" instead of "divorce" if it applies. Most important of all, **have compassion for everyone, including yourself.**

> **Plan what you are going to say, and who is going to say what.** It probably won't go as planned, but if you have talked about it first, then you can feel a little more secure that one or both of you will know what to say. Or what not to say. Also, saying it aloud for the first time without the children present may allow you to cry or feel your feelings before you meet with them. The calmer you are when you speak to your children, the calmer they can be. The more respectful you can each be of the other creates more safety for your children.

Remember that the greatest gift you can give your children is to minimize conflict between you. Much has been written about the aftermath of divorce and how it adversely affects your children. By the time you are ready to have this discussion, you may have exhausted your possibilities of reconciliation. I believe that the most harm to our children comes from the pain we inflict on our spouses. **The more we show compassion and respect, the more we enhance the quality of our children's lives.**

Plan a time that you can have this conversation when you will be available afterwards to process the feelings that may come up for your children. Don't have this talk when your children have to go somewhere right after it's over. You wouldn't tell your teenager before she goes to a party, nor would you tell your younger children right before they leave for school. Sometimes parents have planned to take the children to a park, have dinner together, or do something afterwards that can assure their children that they can all be friendly during and after this process. This may feel impossible to you, so just **structure the timing so that you're both available to your children after the talk.** If it is not possible for you both to be available, then plan who will stay with the children and when the other parent will be able to spend time with them as soon as possible.

Tell your children that you want to talk with them. Sometimes, before you say anything, your children might say, "You're getting divorced." Other times, they know and don't believe it, or feel that if they don't speak about it then it can't be real.

Let them know that you love them and you will both always be there for them. Children get scared at the idea of divorce, just as you do. Knowing that they will always have love from both of you can make them feel safer.

Assure them this is not their fault. Children tend to think they did something wrong or might have caused the break up.

You can say that you have some issues between the two of you that made you both decide you were going to get divorced. Even though one of you might have brought up divorce first, very few people want to be married to someone who does not want to be married to them. Whether you realize it yet or not, there were factors in your relationship that made it difficult for both of you. Probably neither one of you has been happy for a long time.

It is not your children's business to know what those "issues" are. This is where **boundaries** in the discussion are very important. Whether there has been an affair, an addiction, or abuse, it is not necessary to talk about it now (or possibly ever) with them. The reasons are your reasons, and telling them just allows one of you to vent at your children's expense.

They will ask what those reasons are. You can gently, but firmly, let them know that you will not be telling them. You will have to be consistent with this, as they will continue to ask even after the talk. It will often take a great deal of restraint and maturity for you to hold this boundary. You might want to tell them "your side of the story." However, there are always two sides to a story, and the children do not need to be in the middle of it.

Remember that anything negative you say about the other parent reverberates in your children's hearts. Many times, the children take personally what you say about their other parent. A judgment of your spouse implicitly becomes a criticism of them as well.

Tell them that you will always be available to discuss their feelings with them. Let them know that it is normal to feel sad, scared, angry, hurt, and that they can talk to both of you at any time about what they are feeling.

Don't make your children your confidantes. You are there to listen to them, but they do not have to be burdened with your emotions. Many sensitive children take it on as their responsibility to help Mommy or Daddy and "make them happy." This scenario should be avoided at all costs. (Alice Miller's *Drama of the Gifted Child* addresses the issues that arise for children who think they must be caretakers of their parents.)

Let them know that you will take care of yourself and they don't have to take care of you. You can tell them that you are seeing a counselor, have joined a support group, or have many friends who are there to assist you.

Answer their questions that are their concerns. Your children may want to know where they will be living, what school they will attend, who will be leaving the house and when, where will the other parent live, when will the children see the parent who is leaving. To the extent that you know the answers, let your children have this information. Whatever questions are still unanswered, tell them you will let them know as soon as you make those decisions.

Ask them if they want to talk about their feelings now. They may cry, they may yell, they may want to go out and play with their friends. Don't be surprised at any response. Just be there to hear them and to hold them.

When the talk is finished, you can go somewhere in private to process your own tears, or your relief. And then go do something nurturing with your children, or if they are not available, then nurturing to yourself.

One of the hardest parts is over. Now you can live congruently and compassionately. You don't have to hide the reality, and now your children can begin to talk about their feelings, fears, concerns. It will usually be a relief to you because you don't have to hide anything from them anymore.

Your children may have questions in the future. Let them know they can ask you about issues that pertain to them. And keep your boundaries clear. They also may need to see a counselor or join a support group on their own, depending on their age and emotional response to the separation. I have found Rainbows for All Children to be an excellent resource for this purpose.

Rainbows for All Children

Rainbows is an international organization started by Suzy Yehl Marta, a divorced mother of three boys, to help children, parents, and caregivers guide children through divorce, death, and other trauma. Rainbows offers free age-appropriate support groups across the United States and in sixteen other countries, where children can talk about their feelings with other children who are going through the same thing. These groups last six weeks and are facilitated by trained volunteers, and their programs have offered support to more than three million children in the U.S. alone. Check them out at http://rainbows.org

Stay as Loving as You Can

In her book, *The Gifts of Imperfection,* Brené Brown says *"Where we are on our journey of living and loving with our whole hearts is a much stronger indicator of parenting success than anything we can learn in how-to books."*

Do the work you need to do to be as compassionate and loving with yourself as you can possibly be during this difficult time. A healthy parent is the best gift you can give your child. Your children will forever be grateful for the SELF-energy you bring to this process. By minimizing conflict and showing respect in the way you relate to the other parent, you are actually giving your children a gift.

Part of the work of becoming healthy is to let go of resentments, judgments, and blame. You and your spouse have each done the best you knew how to do, and you can move forward with grace. I share the following Intention and Prayer that I wrote for my own divorce many years ago.

Settlement Intention and Settlement Prayer

My **Settlement Intention and Settlement Prayer** were written the night before my divorce was finalized. I gave a version to my husband and our attorneys at the courthouse. I know how it feels to take this journey towards a marital dissolution, and I wanted to remind myself to keep doing all that I could to come from my highest and best SELF and stay loving as much as I could—with my whole heart. I offer these to you with the hope that as you set your intention (and/or pray for support and guidance), you'll be able to influence the process positively—regardless of what your partner chooses to do.

Settlement Intention

I intend to have a peaceful and respectful settlement meeting, in which all parties come together from their Highest Selves, and their own inner guidance and wisdom.

I intend that the Parts of ourselves that are angry, fearful, defensive, revengeful, retributive, punitive, unloving, unforgiving, sad, young, abandoned, resentful, negative, hurting, and hurtful—that all these parts be quelled with the

225

leadership of the SELF, coming from a place of trust in my own presence and light.

I intend to show compassion, forgiveness, gratitude, and appreciation. Although our marriage has come down to a business closing over money and division of assets, I intend that we remember the love that brought us together, and the wonderful children that our union has born. For their sakes as well as our own, I wish to put an end to this process as respectfully and lovingly as possible.

Although we each carry our sadness and pain and mutual regrets, I intend that we can look *beyond* this difficult period to a time when we can be friends and coexist peacefully. I intend that our once-intact family can be rearranged to exist as two intact and loving homes, where our children feel connected and comfortable. I intend that we can hold in a different light the love that once joined us forever; that on the deepest level we wish each other well as we let go.

For the sake of all we once had, and for all we'd planned to share together, let us now finalize the terms of our marital dissolution so that we're both free to get on with our lives.

Let us complete this last painful task with a sense of trust in the love we once shared and, hopefully, can remember after this part is over.

Let us not work from purely simple and self-serving motives, but keep in mind the general welfare of each other and our children.
Let us request our attorneys to contribute whatever is needed for the mutual benefit of all concerned.

In the end, let us know that we behaved civilly, that we can look back with a clear conscience, and that we acted and spoke from our hearts.

Settlement Prayer

I pray for a peaceful and respectful settlement meeting, in which all parties come together from their Highest Selves and their truest connection to Your guidance, wisdom, and love.

I pray that the Parts of ourselves that are angry, fearful, defensive, revengeful, retributive, punitive, unloving, unforgiving, sad, young, abandoned, resentful, negative, hurting and hurtful—that all these parts be quelled with the leadership of the SELF, coming from a place of trust in Your presence and light.

I pray for compassion, forgiveness, gratitude, and appreciation. Although our marriage has come down to a business closing over money and division of assets, I ask that we remember the love that brought us together, and the wonderful children that our union has born. For their sakes as well as our own, I wish to put an end to this process as respectfully and lovingly as possible.

Although we each carry our sadness and pain and mutual regrets, I pray that we can look beyond this difficult period to a time when we can be friends and coexist peacefully. I pray that our once-intact family can be rearranged to exist as two intact and loving homes, where our children feel connected and comfortable. I pray that we can hold in a different light the love that once joined us forever; that on the deepest level we wish each other well as we let go and let God direct our lives.

For the sake of all we once had, and for all we'd planned to share together, let us now finalize the terms of our marital dissolution so that we're both free to get on with our lives.

Let us complete this last painful task with a sense of trust in the love we once shared and, hopefully, can remember after this part is over.
Let us not work from purely simple and self-serving motives, but keep in mind the general welfare of each of us, and our children.

Let us request our attorneys to contribute whatever is needed for the mutual benefit of all concerned.

In the end, let us know that we behaved civilly, that we can look back with a clear conscience, and that we acted and spoke from our hearts.

May You bless us and direct us all. Amen.

Chapter 12
Compassion for ALL

*"The happiness of one's own heart alone cannot satisfy the soul;
one must try to include, as necessary to one's own happiness,
the happiness of others."*
—Paramahansa Yogananda, Indian Yogi

Compassionate Mediation will teach you Compassionate Communication and the Miracle of Empathy so that you'll be able to talk about *all* of your feelings, even the ones you've repressed (or exiled) for years. You'll listen, understand, and have more shared compassion in your relationship.

You'll create healthy and appropriate boundaries as you forgive yourself and your partner. You can accept that you've learned what you're meant to know and can now let go of the past with gratitude and grace.

As you move into your future, you will see that compassion is the healing balm for you and your family. You will relate more "in SELF," and be aware of the higher SELF in everyone, regardless of which Parts they show you.

Compassion for Your SELF

Please remember that you've done the best you could until this moment, and now you can make choices from your true SELF, as you listen to your inner voice, nurture your Inner Child, heal all your wounded parts, and be the Light and Love that you are.

Compassion for Your Children

Minimizing conflict is the biggest gift you can give to your children. You can either learn how to create a new and more loving, respectful marriage with their other parent, or you will be able to create two loving and comfortable homes where they can feel safe and protected. Your friendship can survive as you celebrate birthdays, holidays, graduations, weddings, and grandchildren with more joy and shared connections in the future. You'll learn how to co-parent with gratitude as you count the blessings you continue to share.

Compassion for Your (Ex) Partner

As you keep in mind that you've done the best you knew how to do, you'll realize your partner has also done the same. Your Families of Origin affected your beliefs and behaviors, and you'll learn new ways to react and respond that aren't based on the primal fight-or-flight reaction.

You'll realize that karma plays a role, and that the more positive energy you put into the process, the more positivity will come back to you. Forgiveness is a gift you give yourself (and your family) that will set you free to move on with your life unencumbered from the pain of the past.

Financial gain can cost too much emotionally, but you'll still ask for what you want and need. Your partner has helped you learn important lessons about yourself that will assist you in your next relationship. You'll be able to let go and move on with renewed hope for the future.

Compassion for the Process

Divorce is one of life's main stressors. It is an ending of a relationship, and it needs to be grieved, at the same time that so many life-altering decisions need to be made. You go from being married spouses, to sometime adversaries (as you negotiate your individual needs), to business partners (as you create the financial arrangements), and to co-parents.

Each stage takes time—time to heal, become informed, plan, make decisions. You'll grieve the relationship, the marriage, and the dream. The process takes as long as it takes.

Be good to yourself along the way, and know that you're being guided in the direction of your highest good. Remember to take time to quiet your mind so that you can be in touch with that guidance from within.

Don't rush through to a final document and then wait until later to deal with your feelings. Be compassionate with yourself and everyone involved, and take the time you need to feel balanced, centered, and peaceful (in SELF) as you finalize the details.

And remember to have compassion for the mediator, attorneys, judges, and court personnel who are doing their absolute best to support you, no matter what it feels like at the time.

Compassion for Your Parents

Although your divorce is happening to you, it's also a loss for everyone connected to you. Your parents have made your spouse their child for a very long time. They won't know what to do or how to act, and they'll take their cues from you.

Your parents will want to support you, but they'll also want to stay close to your children and probably to have an amicable relationship with your former spouse too.

You can set the tone for compassion and inclusion. You can quell your parents' fears and concerns if you let them know that your goal is to restructure your family, not destroy it. Remind them that they'll always be able to stay connected to your former spouse, someone they treated as their child. If there are children involved, your parents will have better access to them if they do not have to play any part in an acrimonious battle.

When you model tolerance, forgiveness, and mutual respect, their relief will be palpable. You can teach them how to support *all of you* appropriately, and make room for their feelings, too.

With love, time, and patience, you can all get through this together—feeling supported, loved, and connected in healthy ways.

Compassion for Your Extended Family

As you show your parents how they can handle the conflict, separation, or divorce, your extended families will also learn from you. Holidays will be different as it may not be clear whom to invite. New traditions will be created, and your attitude and energy will foster ones that can bring happiness to everyone.

Their relationship with your spouse will change from "family" to "friend." Blood can be thick, but so is friendship. Respectful relationships with healthy boundaries can be created when your intention is to heal and transform.

When you or your (ex) spouse have a new relationship, other adjustments will also be made. In the future you may each find new partners who are also confident and SELF-led, at least enough to feel comfortable with the presence of your children's other parent for the benefit of all concerned.

Compassion for Your Friends

Just like your family, your friends will be unsure of the role you'd like them to play and how they'll feel about playing it. They'll have their own issues to deal with—their own surprise, loss, feelings of betrayal, and reconnection.

They won't be sure about sharing "custody" of the friendship. How will each of you feel about their spending time with the other? Will you want to know, or not know? How should they treat any new partners in the future? What are the guidelines?

Help your friends feel comfortable about being with each of you and both of you, and again, help them if you can, to be honest about their feelings, too. Your family and friends love you and want to support you, but they may not know what to say or do. No matter how well-meaning they are, no one can make the decision to divorce for you. Your decision and behavior will affect everyone you know for the rest of your life.

Your friends and family will also have adjustments of their own to make. So be compassionate with them and with yourself. It's a difficult time for all concerned.

Compassion for the Next Relationships

As painful and scary as a divorce can be, so is another possible future step for many—"dating."

Take the time to grieve your losses and get to know yourself as a single, empowered, healthy individual. Get to know who you are, without the roles you played in the past. Let your light shine in all the areas of your life you may have neglected—your exercise, meditation, self-care, and fun. Focus on your own personal and spiritual growth.

You will allow yourself to flourish and have the opportunity to attract into your life someone who's healthy, happy, and whole. He or she can be an outer reflection of the inner work you will do to get prepared to meet that special person. You will be able create a wonderful relationship based on all that you've learned from the past.

It takes time, opportunity, and grace. Understand that the process of finding someone new will take as long as it takes. Focus on loving your SELF, and making choices that bring you joy. You will feel more love in your life because of what you bring to it, and owing to that love--eventually, at the perfect time (no matter what you wish otherwise)--that right person for you can appear.

Compassion for the Stepfamily

Patience, patience, patience.

When you're lucky enough to find a new partner, there'll be many adaptations for your new spouse, their children, your children, and your ex. The more "in SELF" you can stay, as each of the participants deals with their own feelings and needs, the sooner peace and harmony can be found.

It's not easy for anyone. Understanding, forgiveness, and love will be your tools for moving into a new relationship that expands your family in healthy ways.

If you are the "ex" watching your spouse remarry, you'll need to be very loving to yourself about the Parts of you that feel jealous, sad, angry, left out, or alone. Staying grateful for your children and being open to a new relationship with their stepparent, you'll find yourself included in more events where you can celebrate what you do have and not be lost in grief over what you don't.

Compassion for the World

Your higher SELF brings you to new heights of consciousness, connection, and compassion for yourself and others.

Your inner peace is one step in the direction of family peace. One step at a time can change the face of divorce, as we know it. Your inner light can help illuminate the world.

Let it shine, let it shine, let it shine.

Afterword—or A New Beginning

September 6, 2000

Pink Light

I sat in the courtroom for our first pretrial, filled with anxiety and dread. I could barely catch my breath. I couldn't think straight. I was afraid of what the lawyers would do, what the judge might say. But most of all, I was anguished by the anger I felt emanating from the man who had once (and for decades) been the center of my life.

I had built my world around trying to please him, just as I had fashioned most of my actions toward receiving praise and approval from others. The sky was falling. My dreams and illusions and life's goals were crashing down around me. I was in divorce court watching my universe explode. The Big Bang. Where would I go from here? But first, how can I cope with being here.

I didn't do so well at that first pretrial.

I probably did as well as anyone else. I didn't throw up. I didn't do bodily harm. I didn't contemplate suicide. So I guess I lived through it. But I did believe there had to be a better way. And by the next time we went to court, I had found it.

I used Pink Light.

I had been given a tool by a friend. And I have passed it along to others. This is a continuation of the torch. Like the Olympics. From one to the other to the other until we take the fire up the mountain, let the light shine, and hopefully help illuminate the world—person by person.

The next time we were in court, I imagined myself surrounded by Pink Light. I put myself in the center of it, and had it protect me. It was an invisible and invincible bubble of safety. I could feel at peace in this light, safe, nurtured. No one could harm me. Nothing could get in. I could watch the proceedings from a detached, witnessing perspective, without being caught up in the proceedings. The drama was someone else's. It didn't affect me.

And when I looked at my husband, hunched in his chair, trying to keep up his Wall of anger and resentment, I sent Pink Light to him. He needed it, as I did. I sent love and forgiveness and peace. I told myself that we were here for a reason and that God was in charge. Whatever happened was God's will. The attorneys could haggle and the judge could rule, but the outcome was part of a bigger plan for our lives. If I got the settlement I wanted, I would be okay. If I didn't, I would still be okay. I would find the guidance in the outcome, and I would be all right. I didn't have to worry and agonize. I would be fine.

The Pink Light was God's Light. It was love. It was acceptance. It was serenity. It was peace.

Safe in my bubble of light, I could forgive my husband and myself. I could forgive both of us for the actions we had taken in the name of divorce self-defense. I could forgive our attorneys for the roles they felt they had to play to fight for our rights. I was at peace. In the middle of the same courtroom, which had previously caused me such dread and foreboding, I sat in gratitude.

The Pink Light had protected me. And even more. I was aware of God's presence, wisdom, guidance and love. This terrible time had become an opportunity to feel a state of grace. I wanted to share it. I wanted everyone to experience it. I wanted the compassion I felt for my husband, myself and everyone that sat in that courtroom (before and in the future), to expand and bring peace.

And now I pass the torch. I talk about the Light. I invite others to use it and feel its safety and protection. Find it in your SELF, and see what I mean.

Now It's Your Turn

You can also practice forgiveness and acceptance of yourself and your partner, and create a new and better relationship— whether a new and improved relationship together, a separation, or a peaceful and respectful divorce. I wish for you an outcome that meets your needs and is a healing and positive transformation for your sake and everyone around you.

I believe that at any time we can either choose love or fear in our interactions. I believe love is always the answer. But it starts with loving yourself.

That is my wish for you. As the Sufi poet Hafiz said, *"When all your desires are distilled, you will cast just two votes: to love more and be happy."* It's my hope for you and your partner that you create a new amazing relationship and a lifetime of peace, love, and joy for you and your family.

From my heart to yours, from my SELF to your SELF, the Divine in me sees and appreciates the Divine light in you. Namaste. I hope to connect with you again soon.

Sending hugs and love,

Linda

Bibliography

Ahlers, Amy and Christine Arylo. *Reform Your Inner Mean Girl.* New York: Atria Books (Simon and Schuster), 2015

Boryshenko, Joan. *Guilt is the Teacher, Love is the Answer.* New York: Grand Central Publishing, 1991

Brown, Brené. *The Gifts of Imperfection: Let Go of Who You Think You're Supposed to Be and Embrace Who You Are.* Minnesota: Hazelden, 2010

Chodron, Pema. *When Things Fall Apart: Heart Advice for Difficult Times.* Boston: Shambhala, 2000.

Chopra, Deepak. *Seven Spiritual Laws of Success.* Novato, California: New World Library, 1994

Chopra, Deepak and David Simon. *Seven Spiritual Laws of Yoga.* Carlsbad, California: Chopra Center Press, 2010

davidji. *Secrets of Meditation.* Carlsbad, California: Hay House, 2012

davidji. *destressifying.* Carlsbad, California: Hay House, 2015

Dyer, Wayne. *Change Your Thoughts—Change Your Life: Living the Wisdom of the Tao.* Carlsbad, California: Hay House, 2009

Ford, Arielle. *Wabi Sabi Love.* San Francisco, California: Harper One, 2012

Ford, Debbie. *Spiritual Divorce.* San Francisco, California: Harper Elixir, 2006

Gray, John. *Staying Focused in a Hyper World.* Mill Valley, California: MarsVenus Heart Publishing, 2014

Hafiz. *The Gift,* translated by Daniel Ladinsky. New York: Penguin Compass, 1999.

Hay, Louise L. and David Kessler. *You Can Heal Your Heart: Finding Peace After a Breakup, Divorce or Death.* Carlsbad, California: Hay House, 2014.

Hendricks, Harville. *Getting the Love You Want: A Guide for Couples.* New York: Harper Perennial, 1990

Kabat-Zinn, Jon. *Wherever You Go, There You Are.* New York: Hachette Books, 2005

Katie, Byron. *Loving What Is: Four Questions That Can Change Your Life.* New York: Three Rivers Press, 2003

Kubler-Ross, Elizabeth. *On Grief and Grieving: Finding the Meaning of Grief Through the Five Stages of Loss.* New York: Scribner (a division of Simon and Schuster), 2007

LaPorte, Danielle. *The Desire Map.* Boulder, Colorado: Sounds True, 2014

Lowrance, Michele. *The Good Karma Divorce.* New York: HarperCollins, 2011

Miller, Alice. *Drama of the Gifted Child.* New York: Basic Books, 1997

Myss, Caroline, *Sacred Contracts.* New York: Harmony Books, 2003

Rankin, Lissa. *Mind Over Medicine.* Carlsbad, California: Hay House, 2014

Rosenberg, Marshall B. *Nonviolent Communication: A Language of Life.* Encinitas, California: Puddle Dancer Press, 2003

Rumi, Jalal al-Din and Deepak Chopra. *The Love Poems of Rumi.* New York: Harmony, 1998

Schwartz, Richard C. *Internal Family Systems Therapy.* New York: Guilford Press, 1997

Schwartz, Richard C. *You Are the One You've Been Waiting For: Bringing Courageous Love to Intimate Relationships.* Oak Park, Illinois: Trailhead Publications, 2008

Simon, David. *Free to Love, Free to Heal.* Carlsbad, California: Chopra Center Press, 2013

Thomas, Katherine Woodward. *Conscious Uncoupling; 5 Steps to Living Happily* Even *After.* New York: Harmony Books, 2015

Williamson, Marianne. *A Return to Love: Reflections on the Principles of "A Course in Miracles".* San Francisco, California: Harper One, 1996

The Guest House

This being human is a guest house.
Every morning a new arrival.

A joy, a depression, a meanness,
some momentary awareness comes
As an unexpected visitor.

Welcome and entertain them all!
Even if they're a crowd of sorrows,
who violently sweep your house
empty of its furniture,
still treat each guest honorably.
He may be clearing you out
for some new delight.

The dark thought, the shame, the malice
meet them at the door laughing,
and invite them in.

Be grateful for whoever comes,
because each has been sent
as a guide from beyond.

—Rumi

"I love helping people calm their minds, heal their hearts, and experience the infinite possibilities that are present in each moment."

As a therapist, mediator, attorney, and teacher of meditation, yoga, and Ayurveda, I have drawn on decades of education and life experiences to help thousands of men and women find peace and balance in their lives. I believe families need not be *broken*, but can be peacefully and respectfully *re-structured*.

I provide online programs to share my tools for increasing the love and compassion you show yourself and others. My clients have improved their lives, created new relationships with their partners, or thrived through divorce with their children safe and their finances, businesses, and hearts intact. I now offer the same to you:

CompassionateCommunicationAcademy.com
Work with me online: www.CompassionateMediationProgram.com
Get your FREE Compassionate Mediation® Toolkit
www.CMToolkit.com
Website: www.LindaKroll.com
Facebook.com/YourCompassionateCommunication
Twitter.com/LindaKroll
Google.com/+LindaKroll
LinkedIn.com/Linda Kroll
Pinterest.com/Lindakroll1
Instagram.com/CompassionateMediation
Connect with your Heart-Centered Community, please visit:
Facebook.com/ HeartCenteredConnections

I look forward to connecting with you.

251

www.ingramcontent.com/pod-product-compliance
Lightning Source LLC
Chambersburg PA
CBHW052032090426
42739CB00010B/1869